welcome to Cyprus

explore the island at a glance...

written by

RENOS LAVITHIS

edited by

ANNA LAVITHIS

TOPLINE PUBLISHING

C welcome to yprus

published by

TOPLINE PUBLISHING
12 The Fairway, New Barnet,
Herts EN5 1HN, England
www.toplineart.co.uk/publishing

A New, Revised and Updated format
of **Explore Cyprus** guide
2008

ISBN: 978 0 948853 01 2

Most photographs have been taken by the author. Others have been
supplied by the Cyprus Tourism Organisation marked as (CTO) and some
from archives, museums and collections, as used by us in previous editions.
Every possible effort is been made to ensure accuracy of information,
but as changes occur occasionally, we apologise for any errors, wrong
information or telephone numbers.

welcome to Cyprus

WELCOME to this *"Earthly Paradise"......"The green jewel of the Mediter-ranean"...... "Supreme in Beauty and well above all other places..."* This is our Cyprus, an island full of History, Culture, Beauty, Hospitality and Life......

A lot has changed since the first edition of our Explore Cyprus guide book was published. The island is now more Cosmopolitan, more commercially involved. The whole place is undergoing a development boom which attracts new peoples, new ideas and new thoughts, all blending with the local traditions and way of life.

In this melting pot of modern 21st century Cyprus, there are are still the old values and hospitality for visitors to appreciate, places of interest which time has left in their original state, and a wealth of scenic, historical, archaeological and natural places to visit and explore.

Above all, Cyprus is now a full member of the European Community and part of the Eurozone currency. That makes the island an integrated part of Europe.

There is still however sadly, the problem of the occupation, division and separation. The northern part of the island is still occupied by Turkey since the invasion of 1974, with a government that no other country has recognised. However there has been some attempt over the years, within local and interna-tional circles, to find a mutually acceptable solution. Because of this and with the recent slackening of border controls which allows greater movement of people between the two sides, one hopes that Turkey may decide to withdraw its troops and allow the local population to find a solution that unites the island.

Due to this relaxation, we felt that it is now time to include some of the well known monuments and places in the north which visitors now have more freedom to visit, but we list them with their old traditional names.

Here, we have tried to give you as much information as possible. We hope this is what you wish to know about Cyprus. We will be delighted to hear your views and we apologise if places and information change, as they do from time to time....

welcome to this enchanting and contrasting island....

enjoy your stay and come back soon......

acknowledgment

I would like to thank my wife Anna for all her enormous input of work in editing, checking and advising on all the text.

Many thanks also go to the Cyprus Tourism Organisation for supplying valuable updated information and photographs, old and new; at the London Office in particular - Orestis Rossides, director, and his assistant Lillian Panayi.

Also the Department of Antiquities, The Cyprus Museum, other Institutions and Collections for their valuable contributions with images and assistance during visits. Thanks also to Chris Granet for all his technical advice. Also Themis Matsangou for all her much appreciated advice.

Finally our gratitude to our distributors in Cyprus, Hellenic Distribution Agency and our UK distributors Gazelle for all their hard work.

contents

PLACES OF
IMPORTANCE
★★★ = Not to be
          Missed

★★ =   Very
          Interesting
          to visit

★ =   Of some
          Interest

get to know Cyprus

SITUATION

The island of Cyprus is situated in the south eastern corner of the Mediterranean close to the coasts of Asia Minor and Syria. It is the third largest (after Sicily and Sardinia) and has an area of 3,572 square miles or 9,250 square kms. Its greatest length, including the long narrow peninsula of Cape Andreas is 140 miles (225kms) and its greatest breadth is 59 miles (94kms).

PHYSICAL FEATURES

A quick glance at the map shows two mountain ranges;

The Troodos range is massive and occupies nearly half the island's total area. Fragmented by geological folding, it is mainly igneous rock with a thicker soil and a covering of pine, dwarf oak, cypress and cedar trees. The highest point is **Mount Olympus or Chionistra** (6,404 feet above sea level) and it is covered with snow during most of the winter months.

The Kyrenia or Pentadaktylos range is composed of limestone with occasional deposits of marble. It forms a narrow belt running the whole length of the northern coast (around 80 miles) and its highest point is Akromandra which is over 3,343 feet above sea level. Between the two mountain ranges is the fertile plain of **Messaoria** (the land between two mountains) which runs from Morphou Bay in the northwest to Famagusta Bay in the east. It is about 80 miles in length and from 15-30 miles in breadth.

There are dozens of rivers in Cyprus but they are without a continuous flow of water. The Coastline is varied, ranging between sandy beaches to rocky coasts interspersed with many bays and capes.

CLIMATE

Cyprus enjoys one of the healthiest climates in Europe with hot dry summers from mid May to mid October and changeable winters lasting from November to early March with occasional rainfall and rare storms. There is plenty of sunshine and on average the sun shines for 330 days a year. The hottest months are July and August. The coastal areas are less unbearable due to the sea breezes and the air is cooler in the mountains. The maximum temperatures reach 33C and a minimum of 6C. In fact during the winter Troodos experiences several weeks of below freezing temperatures at night.

Spring - the season of freshness and beauty when the fields are green and flowers blossom everywhere. A warm and beautiful season with occasional rain.

Summer - as expected is warm and very hot at times. A paradise for all sun lovers. The clouds which appear from time to time are mainly due to the vapourisation of sea water.

Autumn - the end of summer, but the weather is still warm well into November. There is rain at times but it is generally dry and sunny.

Winter - sees snow on Mount Olympus. It is normally cool to cold, particularly at night but warm on sunny days. Rainfall lasts for a few hours but is not regular.

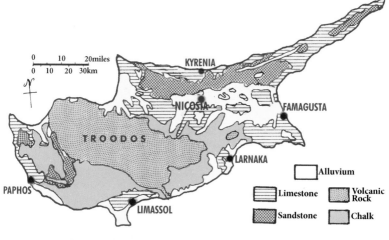

			Alluvium
	Limestone		Volcanic Rock
	Sandstone		Chalk

SPRING

SUMMER

AUTUMN

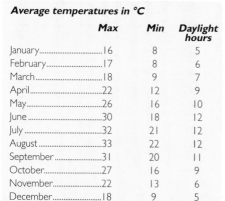

Average temperatures in °C

	Max	Min	Daylight hours
January	16	8	5
February	17	8	6
March	18	9	7
April	22	12	9
May	26	16	10
June	30	18	12
July	32	21	12
August	33	22	12
September	31	20	11
October	27	16	9
November	22	13	6
December	18	9	5

WINTER

THE PEOPLE

The majority of Cypriots are Greek Orthodox Christians (80%) whose origins can be traced back to the great immigrations of mainland Greeks between the 12th. and 10th. centuries BC. The Turkish inhabitants (18%) came to Cyprus after 1571. The other 2% of the population are Armenians, Maronites, Latins and British.
Source: Cyprus Official statistics 1960

However, since 1974 the demography of the island has been altered drastically with the arrival of settlers from mainland Turkey and the presence of an army of occupation in the north of the island. In the Republic, with Cyprus becoming a member of the European Community, the island is experiencing a new influx of British and European workers, business people and retired people who make the island their home.

Latest official population statistics at the end of 2004 show the average population being, Greek Cypriots: 651.100 or 77.8%, Turkish Cypriots: 88.100 or 10.5% (illegal settlers not included). Other Residents: 98.100 or 11.7%. By the end of 2004 the main city population was: **Nicosia** - free area 219.200; **Limassol** - 172.250; **Famagusta** - free area 41.200; **Larnaka** - 77.000; **Paphos** - 51.300

The Family is very strong in Cyprus and it is enlarged by the inclusion of many relatives - second and third cousins. The family circle also encompasses a further number of 'koumbaros' and 'koumeres' - the best men and women at weddings and christenings. There are powerful family bonds.

CUSTOMS AND TRADITIONS

These include religious festivals, some of which have long-standing pagan roots and are very strongly embedded into Cypriot life. Some of the most important are listed here:

New Year's Day - the patron saint is Ayios Vasilios tis Kessarianis (St. Basil of Ceasarea). Many of the beliefs are similar to those of European countries.

Epiphany - on 5th. January, 'Lokomadhes' (doughnuts) are made. There is also the religious ceremony of the blessing of water at a pond, lake, river or by the seashore.

Kataklysmos - A religious festival with very ancient pagan roots (from the days of the rites of Aphrodite) is celebrated all over Cyprus. People gather in seaside resorts to see, hear and participate in the singing and dancing of local folk music.

The Carnival - "Secosis" - This is a series of celebrations, again of pagan origin, to welcome back life in the spring after the darkness of winter and it takes place early in the season. The climax of the festival is reached on the last weekend when the people participate in parades, dancing and singing in carnival atmosphere They also spend the Sunday in an 'orgy' of eating and drinking. This is reversed on the following day **'Green Monday'** or Ash Monday, a day of cleansing and the beginning of the Lenten fast

Easter - "Lambri" - The greatest event of the Cypriot calendar. For a whole week church services reconstruct the last seven days of Jesus life on earth. On Thursday night comes the climax with the arrest and crucifixion of Jesus. Black veils cover the icons and other parts of the church to signify deep mourning for the

Saviour. The burial of Jesus is on Good Friday and this is done in the 'Epitaphios', a carved wooden tomb placed in the middle of the church and decorated by local ladies with all kinds of spring flowers.

Saturday Midnight Mass is the highlight of Easter when the lights go out, the priest then says "Christos Anesti" (Jesus Has risen), the lights come back on and fire works light the skies. On Sunday, families gather together to make 'Souvla' - barbecued lamb, which breaks their long fast. It is, in many ways, the equivalent of the western European Christmas as the time when families travel to be together and celebrate.

August 15th. - Is a celebratory festival for 'Panayia' - the Virgin Mary and in Churches and Monasteries dedicated to her there are celebrations and festivals. August 14th. and 15th. are usually public holidays.

THE DISTRICTS OF CYPRUS

KYRENIA

Kyrenia District

Famagusta District — FAMAGUSTA

Nicosia District — NICOSIA

Paphos District — TROODOS MOUNTAINS — Larnaka District — LARNAKA

PAPHOS — Limassol District — LIMASSOL

Districts and their Capital Towns before the 1974 Turkish Army invasion and occupation of Kyrenia, most of Famagusta and part of Nicosia Districts.

Above: Traditional Easter Bread and popular Flaouna cake bread; Left: Epitafios, decorated with Spring Flowers

9

RECREATION, LEISURE AND ARTS

Sports - Football, tennis and basketball are important for the active Cypriot and facilities and standards are improving all the time. Golf and horse riding has been taken up by a minority especially amongst the younger generation and overseas visitors.

Arts, Poetry, Theatre & Literature - Poetry and tsatista verse-song are a way of life for everyone together with instrumental music. Many villages produce excellent musicians and together with folk dancers, they are part of the national heritage. If music expresses the soul, the dance expresses the emotion of the Cypriot in the same way that flamenco expresses the emotion of the Spanish gypsy.

Musically, it is no surprise that singers such as the former Cat Stevens and George Michael amongst other internationally acclaimed entertainers have Cypriot origins and in Greece, several, mainly female singers, are amongst the most popular and famous artists.

Cypriot **theatre** also has an international reputation. Highly talented companies based in Nicosia perform with great skill and invention both at home and abroad and Literature is widely appreciated.

Fine Art - is very much in the ascendancy and Cypriot artists have achieved great acclaim and stature throughout Europe and America. In proportion to its population, Cyprus has a greater percentage of artists than most other countries. It is a popular art form and widely appreciated. Private Art Galleries exist in all the main towns with the majority being in Nicosia.

Left: The studio and work of one of Cyprus' best known contemporary artists, Andreas Charalambides
Right: Decent from the Cross by G, Georgiou
Below: Ancient Greek Comedy performance ot the Odeon in Paphos

short notes on Cyprus history

8200 - 3900 BC - Neolithic The first inhabitants.
Other settlers came from neighbouring countries. Settlements include Chirokitia; Kalavassos; Cape Apostolos Andreas, mainly around the north and south coasts of the the island.

3900 - 2500 BC - Chalcolithic
Most such communities were found in western Cyprus, where the fertility cults first emerged. Such centres include Lemba and Erimi. The beginning of the usage of copper.

2500 - 1050 BC - Bronze Age
Period of changes; migration; the heroes of the Trojan Wars - many such Greek immigrants arrived on the island, spreading the Greek language, religion and culture. Copper became a valuable trading commodity. The island was also known as Alasia.

1050 - 750 BC - Geometric Period
Many Greek Kingdoms were established such as Paleapaphos - centre of Aphrodite's cult - Salamis, Marion Tamasos, Soloi, Lapithos. Others were under the trading and commercial influence of the Phoenicians - Kition and Amathus.

750 - 475 BC - Archaic Period
Commerce and trade which started in the 8th cent BC continued to prosper and expand. 673-669 - Assyrians controlled the island; 560-545 - The Egyptians under Pharaoh Amasis took control. 545 - The Persians arrived in the island.

475 - 325 BC - Classical Period
Partly under control of the Persians. The trader Phoenicians and the cultural Greeks ruled their kingdoms in semi autonomous power. 411-374 - King Evagoras of Salamis unified the Greek Kingdoms under his influence. Battles between Persians and Greek Kingdoms. Alexander the Great liberated the island from Persian rule.

325 - 58 BC - Hellenistic Years
Under the Ptolemies, the Hellenistic successors of Alexander who established their centre in Egypt. Cyprus became a unified entity, part of the wider Greek World, and adopted all Greek culture, art and customs.

Copper ingot from Engomi, c.1200BC

Salamis coin of Athena

11

58 BC - 330 AD - The Romans
The island became part of the Roman Empire with Paphos as its administrative capital. Its harbour was extended to accommodate Roman fleets en route to Palestine. Saints Paul and Barnabas visited the island, taught Christianity and converted the Roman Proconsul Sergius Paulus to the the new faith, the first such Roman of high rank. Jewish revolt in the island. Destructive earthquakes during 1st cent.

330 - 1191 AD - Byzantium
In 330-395 the Roman Empire was split. Cyprus came under the control of the Eastern Roman Empire, later renamed as Byzantium. The Archbishop of the island obtained Independent status from the early years. - 4th cent. saw destructive earthquakes. 7th & 10th cent - Arab raids destroyed many towns.

1191 - 1192 AD - Richard Lionheart
Isaac Comnenos proclaimed the island for himself. Richard the Lionheart on his 3rd Crusade to the Holy Land arrived on the island, defeated him and took control. Married Berengaria of Navarre in Limassol. In 1192 he sold the island to the Knights Templar.

1192 - 1489 AD - Lusignans
The Templars sold Cyprus to Guy de Lusignan and the island came under a Feudal administrative system, based on that of France with the Catholic Church in control, (the Orthodox Christians being persecuted). Ammochostos - *Famagusta*, became a commercial centre, one of the richest in the Eastern Mediterranean. Great Gothic Cathedrals were built in Famagusta and Nicosia. Genoese controlled Famagusta 1374-1464.

1489 - 1571 AD - The Lion of Venice
Queen Catherine Cornaro ceded Cyprus to Venice The Ottomans took control of most of the Eastern Mediterranean. The Venetians destroyed many important buildings in order to strengthen the defenses; Castles and defensive walls were built in many places.

1571 - 1878 AD - Ottoman Rule
1570 - a turning point in Cyprus' misfortunes. Ottoman Turks landed and captured Nicosia. After a long siege, which was recorded throughout Europe, they took complete control of Famagusta the following year. Greek Orthodox Church reclaimed some of its power. There followed centuries of economic and population decline.

Left: Richard the Lionheart on a stamp;
Right: The Lusignan coat of arms;
Below: The Lion of Venice

1878 - 1960 AD - The British Connection

Britain took over the island's administration; in 1914 Cyprus was annexed by Britain and became a crown colony in 1925. Local unrest to unite with Greece. 1940 - the island escaped the devastating war - volunteers served with the British army. 1955 - Liberation struggle to unite Cyprus with Greece. 1959 - The Zurich agreement was signed and Cyprus Republic was established.

1960 - PRESENT DAY   The Republic

A new nation was created and became a member of the Commonwealth and the United Nations. The first President being Makarios, Archbishop of Cyprus. The established constitution created many problems in both administration and balance of rights which favoured the minority - the Greek community comprised of 78% and Turks of 18%. Separate areas started to appear and the minority retreated into enclaves.

1974 - A military coup to oust Makarios, inspired by the Greek dictators, who ruled Greece at the time, resulted in Turkey invading the island and occupying 37% of the land. Many were killed, 40% of the Greek inhabitants became refugees.

Since the 1980's the Free areas of Cyprus have enjoyed an unprecedented economic and tourist boom with an increased population. In 2004 it became a full member of the European Community.

Since the 1970's continuous efforts have been made from various directions to unify the island. Now there is more intercommunal co-operation and visits across the Green Line are encouraged. Once attitude in some sections of the occupying power accept that the well being of all Cypriots is within a united island, the last barriers will go quickly.

Left: 1878 wood engraving showing the hoisting of the British flag in Nicosia; Below: The first postage stamp issued by the newly formed Cyprus Republic in 1960

Get THE HISTORY OF MODERN CYPRUS written by the late Dr Stavros Panteli and published by Topline Publishing, The ideal book to learn about the island's modern history and the events that formed it. ISBN: 0 948853 32 8

ΚΥΠΡΙΑΚΗ 1960 KIBRIS
ΔΗΜΟΚΡΑΤΙΑ CUMHURIYETI

10 M.

13

Paphos(Pafos)
full of history and traditions

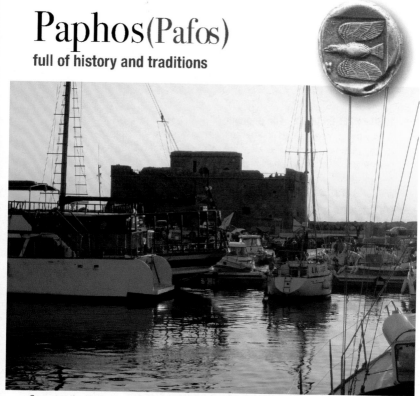

Sunset at the Harbour

The most picturesque resort of Cyprus, Paphos, attracts many visitors and is now a major holiday destination in the Eastern Mediterranean.

It offers charming and beautiful scenery, picturesque mountain villages, hospitable people and a wealth of ancient history and monuments.

In fact, it was the centre of the cult of Aphrodite for a thousand years. It was very important during the Hellenistic Greek periods and was the capital of the island under the Romans.

The town of Paphos is divided into two areas. Sitting on a plateau about 2kms away and overlooking the sea is **Ktima** and **Kato Paphos** with its picturesque harbour which is the main Tourist area.

PAPHOS TOP ATTRACTIONS

Paphos Town offers two Walking Tours:

a- Discover the ancient monuments and glorious past of Paphos (Kato Paphos) which was known then as Nea Paphos...**see map -A-**

b- Explore the old town of Ktima through the market, shopping centre and the Museum.... **see map -B-**

Beach Walks -

a- From the west. Between the hotels and the sea, starting from Azia Hotel walk towards the east and the town. There is a paved walkway.

b- Archaeological Park, outside the fence, from the harbour, along the coast to the bay west of the lighthouse.

c- On the eastern side, along Poseidon Avenue, between hotels along the coast by the sea.

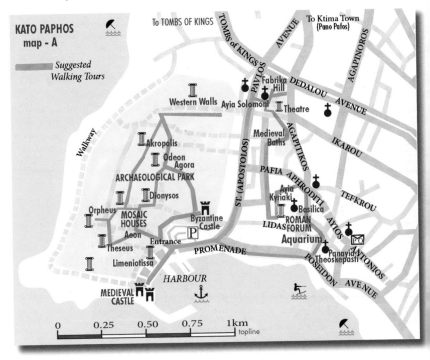

Cyprus Tourism Organisation, Paphos:

Main office - 3 Gladstone Street, Ktima; Tel: 26 93 28 41
Branch - 63 Poseidon Avenue, Kato Paphos; Tel 26 93 05 21
Paphos Airport - Tel: 26 42 31 61 (up to 23.00hrs)
Polis Khrysochous: 2 Vasileos Stasioikou A; Tel: 26 32 24 68

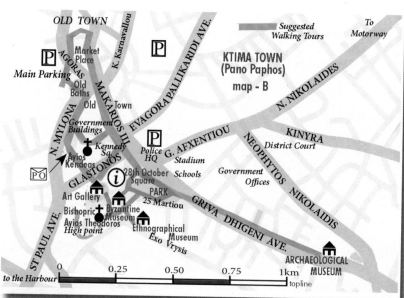

OLD TOWN

Main Parking

Market Place

Old Baths

Old Town

AGORAS

MAKARIOS III

N. MYLONA

K. Karnavallou

EVAGORA PALLIKARIDI AVE.

Suggested Walking Tours

To Motorway

KTIMA TOWN
(Pano Paphos)
map - B

N. NIKOLAIDES

Government Buildings

Kennedy Sq.

Ayios Kendeas

GLASTONOS

PO

Police HQ

G. AFXENTIOU

KINYRA

District Court

NEOPHYTIOS NIKOLAIDIS

Stadium

Schools

Government Offices

28th October Square

PARK

25 Martiou

GRIVA DHIGENI AVE.

Art Gallery

Bishopric

Byzantine Museum

Ayios Theodoros
High point

Ethnographical Museum

Exo Vrysis

ST PAUL AVE.

ARCHAEOLOGICAL MUSEUM

to the Harbour

0   0.25   0.50   0.75   1km

topline

Left: 28th October Square
Below: A local cafe at the market place

16

what to see and what to do
museums and galleries

*Left:
Archaeological
Museum*

*Right: Icon in the
Byzantine
Museum*

ARCHAEOLOGICAL DISTRICT MUSEUM ★★★
43 Griva Dhigeni Avenue; Ktima; **Tel: 26 30 62 15**   Open: Tue-Fri: 08-15.00 / Thur to 17.00/ Sat: 09-15.00 - Parking - Entrance Charge.

In 5 rooms it houses archaeological treasures from most of the ancient local sites. Included is jewellery, coins, pottery, statuettes and statues including some of Aphrodite, from the early years to Byzantine times.

BYZANTINE MUSEUM ★★
5 Andreas Ioannou Street; Ktima; Adjoining the Bishopric. **Tel: 26 93 13 93** Open: Mon-Fri 09-16.00; winter to 15.00 / Sat 09-13.00 - Entrance Charge.

There is a fine collection of religious icons, some from the 12th century plus Gospels, wood carvings and other religious objects.

ETHNOGRAPHICAL MUSEUM ★★
1 Exo Vrysis Street; Ktima;   **Tel 26 93 20 10**
Open: Mon-Sat 09.30-17.00 ; Sun 10-13.00 - Entrance Charge

A private collection in a large old house with exhibits from the Neolithic period to folk objects, costumes, tools and other artifacts. This is well worth a visit.

MUNICIPAL ART GALLERY ★
7 Gladstone Street; Ktima;   **Tel: 26 93 06 53**   Open: Mon-Sun 10-13.00/; Mon-Fri also 15-17.00 (Apr-Oct 17-20.00) - Entrance Free

Mainly paintings from local artists or those living and working in Paphos, including some who are well known.

ancient sites and monuments

MEDIEVAL CASTLE ★★★

Paphos Harbour; Kato Paphos Entrance Charge
Open: Apr-Oct: 08-18.00/ Nov-Mar: 08-17.00

Built in the 13th century by the Franks it was rebuilt by the Turks in 1592. It dominates the southern part of the harbour and offers panoramic views from the top.

ARCHAEOLOGICAL PARK ★★★ UNESCO

Harbour Square; Kato Paphos; **Tel: 26 30 62 17**
Open: Nov-Mar: 08-17.00/ Jun-Aug 08-19.30/ Apr-May & Sep-Oct: 08-18.00
Entrance Charge for the whole park; Facilities;   Parking: nearby car park

Within the Park you visit:

The Mosaic Houses: - These are various Roman houses and villas within a short distance from one another, and the excavated floors have revealed some of the best mosaic scenes in the whole Mediterranean dating to the 2nd and 3rd centuries AD. Some of the houses are covered with a roof for protection from the weather and are a Unesco World Heritage site. They include:

House of Dionysos - The biggest, with many Greek mythological scenes and geometric patterns.

House of Theseus - a large villa, perhaps the governor's residence, with in the centre, the mosaic of Theseus slaying the Minotaur. Other mosaic floors.

House of Aion (Aeon) - The Greek deities parade in various panels, Leda and Swan; Beauty contest between Cassiope and the Nymphs and others.

House of Orpheus - Orpheus charms wild animals by playing the lyre. This is completely covered most of the time for protection.

House of Four Seasons - The four seasons are shown with various animals and geometric patterns.

Above: Ruins from the House of Theseus ; Right: Peneus and Daphne Mosaic

Above: View of the Archaeological Park to the north of the Mosaics showing the Akropolis and the Lighthouse, The Odeon and to its left the remains of the Asklepeion House;

Below: From the House of Dionysos showing Dionysos and Akme drinking wine and Icarios to the right.

Odeon and Agora: - The ancient agora (marketplace) has not been excavated yet and is situated in front of the Odeon, a Greek style ancient theatre which has been partly restored and hosts ancient plays and other theatre performances during summer. Next to it are the ruins of the Asklepeion, the sanctuary of the god of medicine.

Close to the Light House recent studies have revealed the existence of ruins of a Temple dedicated to Arsinoe from the Hellenistic period, unusual for its circular shape.

19

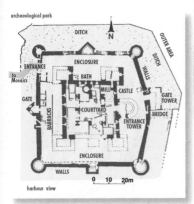

Granite columns (around 40 were counted) at the Byzantine castle and to the left the site plan.

Byzantine Castle (Saranta Kolones): - Overlooking the harbour, in front of the car park. This was built in the 7th century AD to protect the town from Arab raids. It surrendered to Richard the Lionheart in 1191, was then abandoned. Interesting to visit. This is partly restored but most of its granite pillars lie on the ground.

FABRICA HILL ★★

The northern gate where fortifications once stood. It has some rock chambers and observation posts for views of the area.

Ancient Theatre ★★★ is on the south eastern side of Fabrica Hill and has only recently been revealed after years of excavations by Sydney University. It has emerged as the biggest ancient Greek/Roman theatre in the island, seating up to 9.000 spectators. It will take a few more years to finish the work and restore the site to its full glory. Eventually it will be used for performances and cultural events.

AYIA SOLOMONI CATACOMB ★★

Leoforos Ayiou Pavlou; Kato Paphos near Fabrica Hill   Open during daylight; Entrance Free (donation)

This is the the best preserved catacomb in the island, steps lead to underground chambers where a chapel exists. The cavern was a refuge for early Christian believers.

In the small courtyard by the entrance, is a tree which is regarded as holy by locals. It is believed it can cure illness.

Ayia Solomoni Catacomb

Above: A general view of the Byzantine Castle from its courtyard;
Below: The newly discovered and excavated Theatre of Paphos, believed to be the biggest
in the island. There are plans for complete restoration.

TOMBS OF THE KINGS ★★★

2kms from the harbour, along the Coral Bay Road - Tombs of Kings Avenue, Kato Paphos - **Tel: 26 30 62 95**

Open: Nov-Mar 08-17.00/ Apr-May & Sep-Oct 08-18.00/ Jun-Aug 08-19.30
Entrance Charge   Parking and facilities

One of the most unusual and popular ancient sites of the island. It consists of a group of rock cut tombs and chambers, next to the sea, some dating to the 3rd century BC. They were used during the Roman period by early Christians as places of worship and refuge.

There are several types of Tombs, differing in architecture and styles. However, there were no signs that Kings were buried here, more likely high ranking officers and officials.

Above and Below: Two views of Tombs from the site of 'Tombs of Kings' area; Right: Site plan of the Tombs area

ROMAN FORUM - ST PAUL'S PILLAR ★★★

Stasandrou Street, off Leoforos Apostolou Pavlou; Kato Paphos;
Open daily during daylight; Entrance Free

In the grounds of the *Early Christian Basilica* and Ayia Kyriaki church (see under churches).

The Forum is located to the southern part of **Ayia Kyriaki** where there also stands a column to which it is believed, that in 46AD, the Apostle Paul was tied and punished after preaching Christianity. It is called St Paul's Pillar.

To the northern side of the Basilica are the ruins of the once formidable **Gothic Church** erected by the Latins in the 14th century. Renaissance sculptures discovered here are on display at the Paphos Museum.

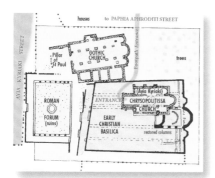 

Above: Plan of the Forum and Basilica; Right: The Pillar to which St Paul was tied and given 39 lashes by the Romans for blinding Elymas when preaching Christianity; Below: The church of Ayia Kyriaki and the ruins of the Gothic church at the front.

23

churches and religious places

EARLY CHRISTIAN BASILICA - AYIA KYRIAKI ★★★

In the same enclosure as the Roman Forum

It was built in the 4th century AD and was one of the earliest churches (Basilica), built over a previous Roman structure, it was a large building. Some floor mosaics survived.

The dominant church was built around 1500 and named *Ayia Kyriaki,* also known as *Panayia Chrysopolitissa* and now functions as an Orthodox church with services also for Anglican (Tel 26 95 30 44) and Catholic(Tel 26 93 13 08) denominations.

PANAYIA THEOSKEPASTI ★★

Dominates the skyline of Kato Paphos; Entrance Free (donations)

Interesting modern church build on the side of the eastern city walls and contains numerous good icons. It commands lovely views.

AYIOS THEODOROS CATHEDRAL Metropolitan Church ★★

Next to the Bishops Palace; Ktima; Open daytime Entrance Free (donations)

Small by the standards of a Cathedral but contains excellent wall paintings executed recently plus a rich interior. The Bishopric building next door is of fine architecture.

Holy Bishopric of Paphos, Ayiou Theodorou St., Ktima - Tel. 26 93 20 92

Above: The interior of the Cathedral of Ayios Theodoros, situated next to the Bishop's Palace Right: Panayia Theoskepasti church, a popular church to visit

other places of interest

THE HARBOUR ★★★

The most popular destination for every visitor. It is colourful, relaxing for walks and having a drink in the numerous cafes. Small fishing boats rest next to pleasure boats and from here you can enjoy a boat trip around the coast of Paphos. In Roman times it was a major port for the fleets en route to the middle east. At that time it extended into a much wider area that included the current car park area.

Experience a Boat Trip from the Harbour......

PAPHOS AQUARIUM ★★

1 Artemis Street; Kato Paphos; Tel: 26 95 39 20 www.tsiolis.com.cy Open: 09-20.00 (winter to 17.00); Entrance Charge. A wonderful marine aquarium with the world of the sea in a spectacular presentation, ideal for all the family.

OLD TOWN - Market Place ★★★

Market Open Mon-Sat (early closing Wed)

The heart of Ktima or Upper Paphos, next to the colonial administrative buildings. The narrow streets of the old shopping centre and the municipal market are popular places that attract many visitors.

Cafes and Tavernas provide local inexpensive breakfasts and lunch; shops offer a variety of souvenirs, jewellry and other interesting items and locals sell fresh fruit and vegetables. A colourful place.

The newly paved Poseidonos Avenue overlooking the harbour as seen in the distance

Shopping in the Old part of the town at the Market place can be a good fun

shopping

The town and surrounding areas offer a number of supermarkets and small local shops catering for all needs. Plus some European and British chain stores are to be found together with numerous Jewellry shops. Located in both the Old Town and the tourist areas all have good buys. The main shopping area is Archbishop Makarios Avenue in the Old Town leading to the Market Place.

Cyprus Handicraft Centre - Government funded to encourage local crafts is worth a visit: Leoforos Apostolou Pavlou No 64   Tel: 26 30 62 43

swimming - water sports

The coastal areas of Paphos Town do not offer the desired sandy beaches and shallow water but there are coves and small areas in front of hotels (which are open to all the public). Some provide umbrellas and sunbeds for a fee. Here you will also find numerous watersports which are licensed by the local authorities, if in doubt please check.

Most such beaches and watersports are to be found along Poseidon Avenue and up at the far end where there is a *Public Beach run by Geroskipos* municipality offering various facilities Tel: 26 23 45 25.

Best beaches are in *Coral Bay* some 9kms (7 miles) to the west of town.

*Above: Watersports at Paphos;
Right: The long beach at Polis*

The famous Geroskipos delights, tasty and aromatic

EXCURSIONS
classical tour

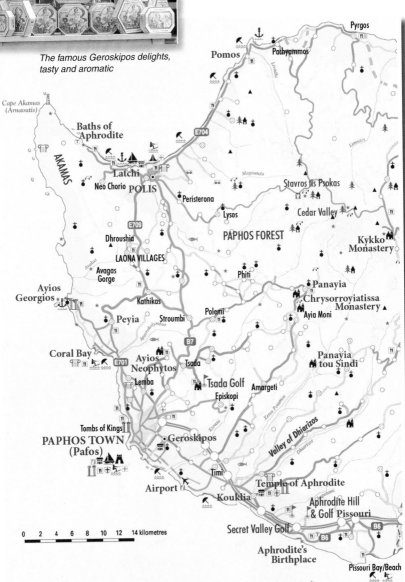

Pyrgos

Pomos   Pachyammos

Cape Akamas
(Arnaoutis)

Baths of
Aphrodite

E704

AKAMAS

Latchi

Neo Chorio   POLIS   Stavros tis Psokas

Peristerona

Lysos   Cedar Valley

E709   Dhroushia   PAPHOS FOREST   Kykko
Monastery

LAONA VILLAGES

Avagas
Gorge   Phiti   Panayia

Ayios
Georgios   Kathikas   Chrysorroyiatissa
Monastery

Peyia   Stroumbi   Polemi   Ayia Moni

B7

Coral Bay   Panayia
tou Sindi

E701   Ayios
Neophytos   Tsada

Lemba   Tsada Golf   Amargeti

Episkopi

Tombs of Kings

PAPHOS TOWN   Geroskipos
(Pafos)

Timi

Airport   Temple of Aphrodite

Kouklia

Aphrodite Hill
& Golf Pissouri

B6

Secret Valley Golf   B6

0 2 4 6 8 10 12   14 kilometres

Aphrodite's
Birthplace

Pissouri Bay/Beach

27

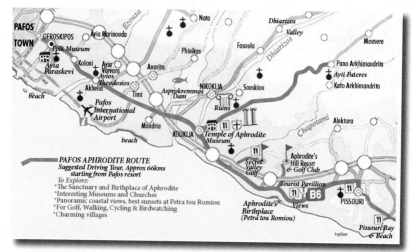

GEROSKIPOS / Folk Museum / Old Church ★★★

A large village to the east of Paphos town, nearly joined now, once known as the Holy Gardens of Aphrodite, is also famed for its Delights (sweet Cypriot Delights) with unique ingredients and taste.

A few minutes walk from the square is the **Museum of Folk Art** with an interesting collection: **Tel 26 30 62 16** Open: Daily- Nov-Mar: 08-1600/ Apr-Oct: 09-17.00   Entrance Charge

On the southern site of the village square is the church of **Ayia Paraskevi,** originally build in 843AD it is a five domed Byzantine structure with a rich interior.   **Tel: 26 96 18 59**

Open to public Mon-Sat: 08-13.00 & 14-16.00 (Apr-Oct to 17.00
Entrance Free (donation) Parking around the square. Cafes and tavernas

*Ayia
Paraskevi
Church at
Geroskipos*

KOUKLIA VILLAGE(Ancient site of Paleapaphos) / Temple of Aphrodite /Museum / Old Church ★★★

14kms(9miles) to the east of Paphos Town, just off the old main highway to Limassol. Built on a plateau overlooking the fertile land below, facing towards the sea, Kouklia was an important Kingdom in ancient times. It once resisted Persian rule and was captured after a long siege. It was also the centre of Sugar Production in Medieval Times. Remains of the sugar mill are to be seen to the south. It has a number of tavernas around the square for evening meals. From there you can visit the site of:

The SANCTUARY OF APHRODITE where once stood the formidable Temple of Aphrodite and where the cult of Aphrodite was practised for over 1000 years. The Temple was established around the 11th cent. BC by Agapenor. It subsequently grew into an important religious centre which also became the political base of the Kingdom of Paleapaphos (This was transferred to modern Paphos, then called Nea Paphos by the Ptolemies around 300BC).

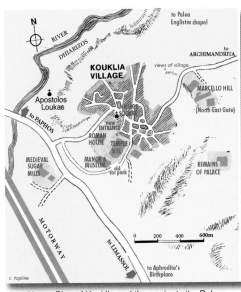

Above: Roman coin showing the Temple Altar; Below: The plan of the Temple

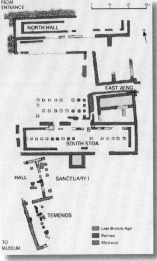

Above: Plan of Kouklia and the ancient site; Below Panayia Katholiki Church

The worship of Aphrodite was one of the most important cults in the ancient Greek world and celebrations took place every spring with pilgrims gathering in Geroskipos from all the known world.

From the Holy Gardens of Geroskipos, a 7 mile procession to the Temple was part of the whole ceremony which continued with the arrival of the worshippers at the Temple.

The remains are a small reminder of what was once a large Temple. Many of the finds from the site and surrounding areas of the ancient town are to be seen at the small museum which is housed in the **Medieval Manor** which has now been restored. It is situated to the southern part of the temple site.

Sanctuary Site and Museum: Tel 26 43 21 80

Open daily 09-16.00 (Thur to 17.00) except on holidays;   Entrance Charge

On the eastern site of the ruins is the small church of **Panayia Katholiki** also known as Panayia Galatariotissa (our Lady the Milk Giver), also know as "Panayia Aphrodissa", it was used by the Latins who were resident at the Manor House.

Above: A view of part of the remains of
Aphrodite's Temple
Right: The Sacred Stone – Cone of
Aphrodite's Temple is exhibited in the small
museum;

30

APHRODITE'S BIRTHPLACE (Petra tou Romiou) - ★★★
The Rock of the Greek

"The moist breeze of zephyr brought her there

(to Paphos shores) on the waves of the sea

with a noise of thunder among the soft foam.."

That is how Homer described the birth of Aphrodite at this spot known now world wide as the Birthplace of Aphrodite, the Goddess of Love...An impressive rock formation on the edge of the water by a pebbled beach.

High above the rock, views either from the side of the road or the Tourist Pavilion Cafe-restaurant are spectacular and the sunsets must not be missed.

Lower down there is a parking area and a small cafe with facilities and a short tunnel leads to the rock. Bathers should be aware of currents and deep areas.

A place for romantic couples but also for lovers of myths and legends.

Open during daylight; Entrance Free. Keep the place tidy.

Romantic Aphrodite's Birthplace, also known as Petra tou Romiou, painted by Renos Lavithis (see www.renosart.co.uk)

31

Above;
Panoramic view
of Petra tou
Romiou
(Aphrodite's
Birthplace) at
sunset,
Right: The golf
Course at
Aphrodite Hill
village resort

APHRODITES HILLS VILLAGE/ A tourist resort with a difference ★★

Half way between Kouklia Village and Aphrodite's Baths, high above the hills is a new town that has been built by the enterprising Lanitis family. It is a Tourist town with luxury villas, houses, a hotel, health and recreation facilities and a beautifully landscaped Golf Course.

PISSOURI BEACH ★★

A haven of a tourist retreat, this long shingle beach is a short drive from Pissouri Village with its narrow old streets and traditional atmosphere.

The beach provides many water sports, ideal for surfing and boat trips. Numerous tavernas and the hotel are ideal for excellent eating and refreshment.

inland to mountains

PANAYIA TOU SINDI ★★★

5kms from Pentalia village, it is best reached with an organised guided tour or jeep safari excursion as only an unsurfaced road connects this isolated old monastic complex which was abandoned.

It lies on the banks of Xeros River. Once it must have been a large medieval monastery which has recently been restored with funds from Europa Nostra.

THE VALLEY OF DHIARIZOS ★★★

Along the river of Dhiarizos, now dry due to the dam built further up to retain the water, in ancient times it was full of sites extending from Kouklia (Paleapaphos) which is to the south. Now there is nothing to be seen but dreams for archaeologists....It is a picturesque trip through the small villages dotted all around the valley and high up the mountains to the north on the way to Platres.

Near the village of Ayios Georgios, over the other side of the river - some 3miles to the east are the ruins of **Ayios Savvas tis Karonas**, once a large Monastic settlement, inhabited by Latin monks, now abandoned.

-7- Pretori/Nelion Winery - Tel: 25 44 24 45/ 99 66 64 14 (see map p27)

At the start of the trip before Nikoklia village is the **Dam of Asprokremmos**, which is of interest to some.

FOREST OF PAPHOS ★★★

Best reached from Panayia village or Kannaviou over unsurfaced roads, or even better with an organised Safari Excursion. This is majestic, cool, inspiring and the part of the forest with the Cedar Trees is even more fascinating.

In the heart of the forest is Stavros tis Psokas, 55kms from Paphos Town, with a Forestry Station and a youth hostel. Also kept here, in a protected enclave, is the shy, elegant and rare symbol of Cyprus, The Mouflon.

Panayia tou Sindi old monastery (Exalt Travel)

Wine Villages of Paphos

Situated in the central areas surrounded by hills, mountains and valleys are the traditional villages that produce the wine.

PANAYIA VILLAGE ★★

Panayia is a lovely village at the edge of the forest with panoramic views. It is also known for being the birthplace of Archbishop Makarios (1913-1977), first President of the Republic of Cyprus - Here is a small museum about his life in the place that he was born, open daily 10-13.00 and 14-18.00

-3-Vouni Winery/ Panayia: Tel: 26 72 27 70

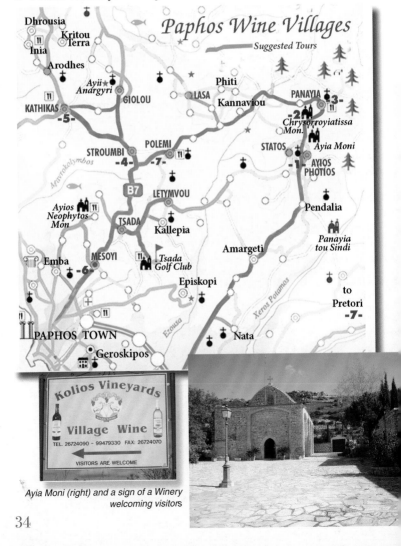

Ayia Moni (right) and a sign of a Winery welcoming visitors

CHRYSORROYIATISSA MONASTERY ★★★

To the south of Panayia, 40kms from Paphos town. An enchanting monastery built on the side of a mountain with commanding views of the valleys below..

The church is of great interest as is the rich collection of Holy Books and religious Ornaments some of which can be viewed at the ***Icons and Treasures Museum*** -Daily 09.30-12.30 & 13.30-18.30 (Sept-Apr to 16.00) Monastery opens Daily.

Tel: 26 72 24 57   Entrance to church is Free (donation); to museum, a charge.; From the shop you can purchase the good wine which is made in the monastery wineries. Parking outside by the square.

-2- Monte Royia Winery at Monastery: Tel: 26 72 24 57

A couple of Kms down the road is to the south there is another similar monastic establishment, that of **Ayia Moni** (The Holy Monastery), built on an ancient site and with an interesting church.

-1- Kollios Winery / Ayios Photios - Statos area:
Tel:26 72 40 90

The majestic monastery of Chryorroyiatissa courtyard. To the left is the entrance to the church, to the right are the museum and shop selling icons and local wines

Tsada with a golf club and the monastery of **Stavros tis Minthas,** a restored old monastic complex. **Polemi,** a village with interesting churches;

-7- Sodap main district winery at Polemi
-6- Figardos Winery/ Mesoyi Village: Tel: 26 94 98 14

Phiti, in the old days a centre of traditional embroidery, now revived with the establishment of a *Weaving Museum*. Open Mon-Sat: 08-12.00 & 14-17.00 (Nov-Apr: after. 13-15.00) **Tel 26 73 21 26.** Entrance Free - items for sale

In the heart of the wine areas are **Stroumbi** and **Giolou** villages along the highway to Polis and main wine centres,

On the western side are the *Laona Villages* which include **Kathikas**, a large village with narrow streets and old houses.

-4- Kamenterena Winery/ Stroumbi Village: Tel: 26 33 00 00
-5- K&K Vasilikon Winery/ Kathikas Village: Tel: 26 63 32 37

Arodhes with its old traditional houses; **Inia** with beautiful surroundings and a *Folk Art Museum*, mainly of Basket weaving which opens till sunset: Mon-Sat 11.00-13.00 (also Jun-Sept 16-19.00 but Oct-May 14-17.00.) **Tel: 26 33 25 62** Entrance Charge

Most important of all is **Dhroushia,** an ideal centre to stay is the local hotel and to use it as a base to explore the surrounding countryside. It has an interesting *Weaving Museum* which open Mon-Sat: 08.30-12.00 (Mon-Fri also 14-16.00) **Tel: 26 33 25 61** Entrance Charge

Phiti museum of Weaving and Embroidery a the village square showing exhibits and the keeper at work

north western Paphos - road to Akamas

AYIOS NEOPHYTOS MONASTERY / Museum ★★★

9kms north of Paphos Town. Situated in beautiful surroundings, it was founded by Ayios (Saint) Neophytos in the 12th century, a hermit who searched for the ideal place to settle and and isolate himself from people.

Here he built his own living quarters by cutting caves out of the rock high up, called **The Enclistra,** where he lived, wrote books and hymns about the Faith and preached to his followers who used to gather below. The living quarters have a courtyard with small gardens and the church is next to it, dedicated to the *Virgin Mary*. It is worth a visit as it contains excellent frescos and beautifully executed icons.

Tel: **26 65 24 81**   Parking below by the kiosk and shop

Church open during daylight when there are no services, Free (donation) - Enclistra and Museum of religious relics is charged-Open: Apr-Oct 09-13.00 & 14-18.00 (Nov-Mar to 16.00)

Left: Plan of the Enclistra;
Above: Panoramic view of Ayios Neophytos monastery (CTO).
The Enclistra is at the far end-left

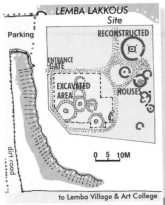

Above: The sculptures at the front of Lemba Art College; Below: The site of Lemba Lakkous ; Left: Site map of Lemba Lakkous Chalcolithic site.

LEMBA VILLAGE / ART COLLEGE / ANCIENT SITE ★★

This small village on the upper road to Coral Bay is the centre of the *Cyprus College of Art*, now included in many itineraries due to its amazing wall of sculptures which is the work of many artists who passed through the college over the years.

On the south western edge of the village, is the Chalcolithic site of *Lemba Lakkous* dated to c3500BC. The area is fenced but can be observed from the sides (if the gate is closed). Some round houses have been reconstructed by using information uncovered and they show examples of prehistoric buildings.

CORAL BAY/ BEACHES / ANCIENT SITE ★★★

The best beaches of Paphos are around here, some 9km from Paphos Town, but be aware, they get crowded over the summer months.

The road leading to the Bays has now expanded into a tourist town with shops, tavernas, bars and coffee shops.

In the central peninsular between the Bays is the ancient site of -

Maa Paleokastro. A Museum of the Mycenean Greek Colonisation of the island, it is built in unusual architectural style. Pass the Thalassa Hotel on the western side to reach it.

Open Daily: 08.30-17.00 (Apr-Oct to 18.00)   Entrance Charge.

Above: The entrance to the Mycenean Museum at
Maa-Paleokastro and Left a site map;
Below: A panoramic view of Coral Bay

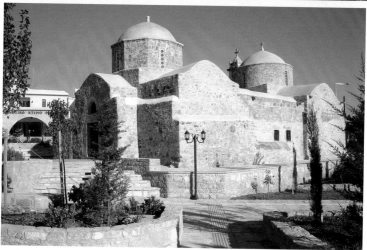

Panayia Chryseleousa church at Emba village centre, a popular church to visit

AYIOS GEORGIOS PEYIAS /Basilica / Church / Cape Drepanon ★★★

Peyia is a village north of Coral Bay. From the top above the village the views of the coastline are breathtaking. The village itself has been expanded and is a very popular place for many British residents.

Just about 5kms west of Peyia is the old Roman settlement of Ayios Georgios Peyias. For many years a fishing harbour, it is now a tourist centre named after Saint Georgios, the guardian of fishermen. It is dominated by the **Church of Ayios Georgios** in the middle of the square. When open you may visit free of charge and pray if you so wish.

Below the church is the small fishing harbour and the coast is dominated by **Geronissos** Island which is close to the shore. Neolithic and Roman habitation was discovered on the island.

To the north of the square is the fenced, ancient site of Christian remains that were built on the site of a formidable Roman settlement. Excavations unearthed 3 churches including a 6th century AD Basilica. Floor mosaics and restored low walls can be viewed.

Archaeological site of Ayios Georgios (Basilica)

Open Daily: 08.30-17.00 (Apr-Oct to 18.00)   Entrance Charge.
Parking by the square. Road down to beach and harbour. Fishing trips can be arranged from there. Tavernas serving fish and other specialities.

SNAKE GEORGE (Reptile Park) ★★

Along the road on the way to Ayios Georgios Peyias, is a fascinating collection of over 100 snakes and reptiles from the island.
Open: daily 10am to sunset **Tel: 99 98 76 85** www.snakegeorge-cy.com
Entrance Charge

BIRD & ANIMAL PARK ★★

Along the road to Ayios Georgios Peyias. A paradise of local and migratory birds. Open daily 09 a.m. to sunset.
Entrance Charge www.pafosbirdpark.com **Tel: 26 94 58 25/ 99 56 39 47**

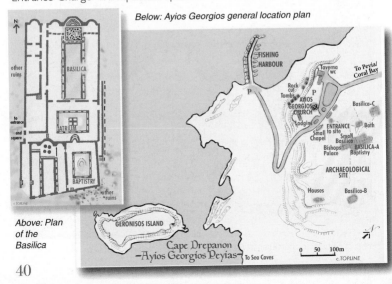

Below: Ayios Georgios general location plan

Above: Plan of the Basilica

40

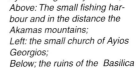

Ayios Georgios Peyias area;
Above: The small fishing harbour and in the distance the Akamas mountains;
Left: the small church of Ayios Georgios;
Below; the ruins of the Basilica

41

AVAGAS GORGE ★★★

Unique in the island, this dramatic geological phenomenon is explored from either the coastal area west of Ayios Georgios Peyias or from the south of Arodhes village in the Laona area.

The Gorge is about 2kms in length along a steep sided valley with spectacular cliffs on both sides and with large rock formations, most impressive being the southern part. It needs special walking shoes and is for fit people only. It is better explored with an organised group such as Exalt Tours and safari excursions.

AKAMAS NATIONAL PARK ★★★

West of Ayios Georgios Peyias is the wilderness of Akamas. It is a beautiful place that has been left just as nature provided.

The coastline is full of exciting rock formations, bays and inlets and the sandy beach of Lara is a preservation area for the breeding of Turtles.

Some hilly inland areas are the habitat of numerous wild flowers and birds.

For adventures, you need a 4 x 4 car which can take you over a rocky, unpaved road a few kms westward. More can be achieved with an off road car such a jeep, or better still, explore the area by joining a specialist safari or excursions tour.

Do not be surprised if occasionally you may come across British soldiers in training as a special agreement allows them to do so. If you venture on the trip, make sure you have plenty of supplies such as water and food and avoid staying after sunset and becoming lost.

EXPLORE THE WILDERNESS OF THIS BEAUTIFUL AREA - TAKE CARE OF THE TURTLES.......

Cyclamen – a flower to be seen in Akamas

Panoramic view of the Akamas Coastline- Khrysokhou Bay area (CTO)

THE ROAD TO POLIS
Suggested Driving Tour from Pafos Town. Approx 86kms
To Explore:
*Stunning and changing scenery, from vineyards to hill
  resorts and down to Khrysokhou Bay and coast
*Picturesque villages, old churches & small museums
*Nature Trails and Cycling
*Flora and Fauna is abundant

to Pomos
beach

Cape
Akamas
Arnaoutis

Fontana Amoroza

E704

Ayios
Georgios Island

Khrysokhou Bay

Arkaka

Baths of Aphrodite
Tourist Pavillion

beach

Makounda

Ayios Konon
Ruins

beach

Fishing
Harbour

Ancient
Marion

POLIS

Kopos
Isle

Latchi

Museum

Smiyies

PRODROMI

Pelathousa

Tjioni
Island

Ayios Minas

NEOCHORIO

Khrysokhou

Steni

Androlikou

Goudhi

Peristerona

Kholi

Museum

Skoulli

Panayia
tou Flou

Phasli

E709

Ayia
Ekaterini

Terra

Kato Akourdalia

Turtle
Hatchery

DROUSIA

Museum

Inia
Museum

Pano Akourdalia

Kritou
Terra

Miliou

Avakas

Kato Arodhes
Pano Arodhes
Museum

LAONA

Ayii
Anargyri Spa

YIOLOU

AVAGAS
GORGE

KATHIKAS

Theletra

Fishing Harbour

Views

STROUMBI

Geronissos
Island

Ayios
Georgios
Peyias

Basilica
Bird Park

Akoursos

Mavrokolymbos

Reptiles

PEGIA

Sea Caves

New Town

Kili

CORAL BAY

B7

Maa Paleokastro
Museum

beaches

Ayios
Neophytos
Monastery

E701

Museum

TSADA

WESTERN COASTAL ROUTE
*Suggested Driving Tour of Approx.
return trip of 46kms*
To Explore:
*Fishing harbours, beaches & coves
*Contrasting Coastline, rocky & sea caves
*Byzantine Churches and Monastery
*Traditional picturesque villages
  with local museums
*Ideal walking & Cycling
*Ancient Sites
*The wilderness of Akama natural park

New Town
Kissonerga

Tala

Trimithousa

MESOYI

Art
College
Ancient Site

Lemba

EMBA

Stavros
Minthas

Tsada
Golf
Club

Church

CHLORAKAS

Anavargos

Armou

PAFOS

Konia

Tombs
of Kings

TOWN

GEROSKIPOU

If you drive into Akamas
use suitable cars as the road is rough
and difficult for ordinary cars
ALLOW EXTRA TIME FOR THIS JOURNEY

topline

Harbour

*The Avagas
Gorge (Exalt
Tours)*

*Typical coastline
of Paphos*

the bay of Chrysochou (Khrysokhou)

POLIS / Town / Museum / Beach ★★★

37kms north of Paphos Town

Tourist Information Office: 2 Vasileos Stasikou Street Tel: 26 32 24 68

Once the Kingdom of Marion, founded in the 10th cent BC and renamed by Ptolemy Philadelphus around 285BC as Arsinoe. Excavations on the eastern and northern sides revealed various items which are in the Museums of Nicosia and Paphos, others are to be viewed at the **Marion Archaeological Museum:** 26 Makarios 3rd Avenue **Tel: 26 32 29 55** Open: Tue-Fri 08-15.00 (Thur to 17.00)/ Sat 09-15.00 Entrance Charge

The town is now a tourist centre and attracts numbers of visitors due to the beauty of the area, the close proximity of the coast to the north and to the idyllic coastline of Aphrodite's Baths

The Beach is long and mostly empty with some facilities around the Camping Site. The town centre, mainly pedestrianised, offers shops, cafes and tavernas. The church of **Ayios Andronikos** has some interesting wall paintings, worth visiting when open, usually on Mon. Tue. Wed and Fri - Entrance Free (donation)

Ayios Nicholas Church: Catholic Mass c/o Tel: 26931308

Polis also offers the interesting **Byzantine Museum of Arsinoe** housed in the Bishopric Palace of Arsinoe, situated in the village of Peristerona, 9kms to the south of Polis. **Tel: 26 35 25 15** Open- Mon-Fri: 10-13.00 & 14-18.00 (Nov-Mar to 16.00)/ Sat: 10-13.00 Entrance Charge; Parking

Ayia Kyriaki church – Polis   Above Right: Map plan of the Centre of Polis

Old part of Polis Town Centre with its old houses and the relaxing cafes

Above: Eating Fish at Latchi Harbour - the perfect place;
Right: The popular Baths of Aphrodite – Pool.

LATCHI ★★★

The famous seaside resort with its fish tavernas and a fishing harbour which attracts many visitors. It has recently been renovated and expanded.

Boat trips can be arranged from here along the bay and as far as the northern coast of Akamas peninsular and to the beautiful spot of the *Blue Lagoon* at the top end. Fishing trips can also be organised. A number of water sports are available on the beach along Latchi area.

BATHS OF APHRODITE ★★★

This is one of the most popular beauty spots in the island which attracts many visitors. It is at the end of the main road from Polis through Latchi with parking by the Tourist Pavilion which serves meals and refreshments. The views from here are spectacular and the walk to the semi cave - pool is rewarding. It was here, according to the Legend that Aphrodite used to come with her lovers to bathe in the cool spring in such peaceful surroundings.

For the energetic, there are numerous walks on **Nature Trails** organised by the Cyprus Tourism Organisation, all presented in a well produced booklet. Visit www.visitcyprus.org.cy for full details

One such place reached only on foot or by boat along the northern part of Akamas peninsular, **Fontana Amoroza** (Spring of Love) was idealised by the poets and writers of Medieval times.

POMOS ★★

North of Polis, driving along the bay with its numerous villages on one side, shingle beaches on the other. These are mainly empty but be aware of steep, sharp drops, there is also the occasional taverna. Pomos is not an attractive village except for the surrounding area and the rocky coastline.

On the northern side and the following the Bay, a small fishing harbour is an ideal stop over on the way further up to **Pachyammos** with its commanding church of **Ayios Raphael.** Further to the north is the isolated village of **Pyrgos,** ideal for explorers.

View of the Khrysokhou Bay from the Tourist Pavilion at Baths of Aphrodite area

useful telephones

Urban Bus Co................ 26 93 44 10
Inter-city Bus Co.............26 93 68 22
Paphos-Polis Minibus... 26 93 68 22
Inter-city Taxi Express...26 93 31 81
Local Transport............. 26 93 42 52

First Aid................ .... 26 80 31 45
Paphos Hospital........ .. 26 80 31 00
Polis Hospital.................. 26 82 18 00
Private Doctors.. 1426
Ambulance/Fire/Police 199 / 112
Night Chemists.... .... 1406, 90 90 14 16
Droushia Health 26 33 23 23
Panayia Health 26 72 23 57
Pomos Health 26 34 23 38
Pyrgos Health 26 52 23 53
Salamiou Health 26 44 22 22

Phiti Health 26 73 22 95

Forest Fires..................... 1407
Police Headquarters...26 80 60 60
Police Office....................26 30 61 48
Fire Service.......................26 80 62 92
Airport Fire....................26 30 65 40
Post Office.......................26 30 62 21
Harbour Customs...... .26 94 68 40
Antiquities...,,,,,,,,,,,,,.......26 93 25 54
Paphos Town Hall........26 93 21 16
Water Authority...........26 93 23 74
Electricity...........................26 84 11 00
Paphos Airport..............77 77 88 33
Religious Services
Anglican Church..........26 95 30 44
Catholic Mass.................26 93 13 08
German Evangelical Ayia Kyriaki Church
Catholic Mass at Polis 26 93 13 08

distances

from Paphos town to:	kms	miles
Limassol.............................	68	42
Nicosia..........................	149	93
Larnaka................................	139	87
Troodos (via Limassol)	113	71
Ayia Napa........................	175	109
Paralimni/Protaras........	179	111
Polis...................................	35	22
Larnaka Airport.............	140	87
Paphos Airport................	15	9

The picturesque fishing inlet at Pomos area, a place to try local fish

activities -

Island Cove Theme Park - *For all the family* -mini golf - close to Poseidonos Avenue, opposite hotels, eastern side.   Tel: 26 99 11 77
Open all year: Entrance Charge   email: land.cove@cytanet.com.cy
Aphrodite Waterpark - *For all the family* - eastern side of hotels area off Poseidon Ave below Geroskipos - refreshments, eating, facilities.
Entrance Charge.   Open: May - October Tel: 26 52 72 11
email: info@aphroditepark.com web: www.aphroditewaterpark.com
George's Ranch -Horse Riding Club Peyia Tel: 26 62 10 64

PAPHOS GOLF
Cyprus Golf Resorts : Tel: 26 64 27 74
Tsada Golf Club - 18 holes - par 72 - 6060m
Secret Valley - 18 holes - par 72 - 5904m   For both cyprus golf resorts:
email: golfers2@cytanet.com.cy   web: www.cyprusgolf.com

Aphrodite Hills Golf - 18 holes - par 71 - 6269m - only with buggy
Tel: 26 81 87 00   email: golfreservations@aphroditehills.com.
web: www.aphroditehills.com/golf

Limassol(Lemesos)
the cosmopolitan city

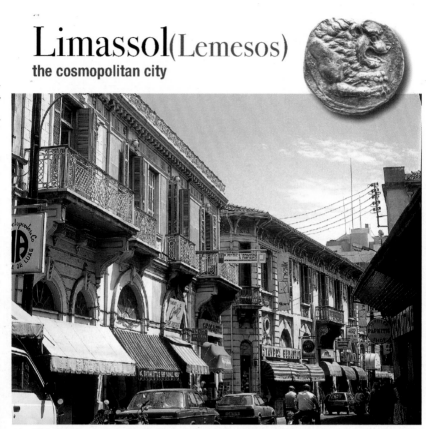

The shopping main street of Ayiou Antoniou in the old town (CTO)

The island's second largest town with an estimated population of around 180,000 including the suburbs. It is the most important commercial city with a large harbour.

It has many hotels, holiday apartments, shops, restaurants, and entertainment places to amuse you all night. With such a contrasting life it has become unique for its cosmopolitan atmosphere.

It has developed into a high quality holiday destination with top hotels, easy access to all other Cyprus resorts, good shopping centres and lovely beaches along the Bay.

LIMASSOL TOP ATTRACTIONS

Limassol Walking Tours:

a - Walk around the old town, along the promenade, the Medieval Castle, the shopping areas of Ayios Andreas - all at your own pace and in your own time
b- Join an organised walking tour with a guide; information from the Limassol Tourist Offices

(i) - Old Limassol - start CTO Office Tel: 25 36 27 56

(ii) - Tour of Germasoyia - bus & walking tour (Oct.-April) Starts at the Tourist Area Tel: 25 32 32 11 - This is organised on alternate dates of the week.

Beach Walks

In the tourist area there is a long paved walkway between the hotels and the sea that runs all the way to the ruins of the ancient site of Amathus,

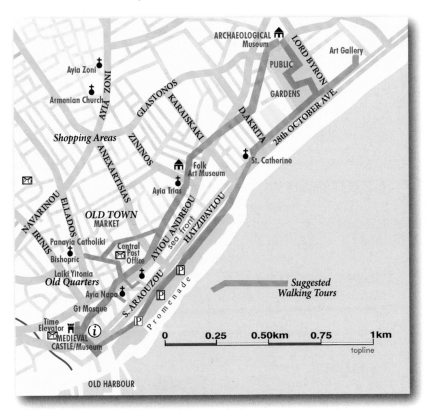

Limassol Tourist Information Offices
Main Office: 115 Spyrou Araouzou Str. Tel: 25 36 27 56
Harbour Office: 25 57 18 68
Germasoyia Tourist area: 22 Georgiou A' Str. Tel: 25 32 32 11

what to see and what to do
museums and galleries

Left: Head of Zeus from Fasoulla village;
Above: Pot from Amathus site; Both of 6th
cent BC, exhibited at Limassol Museum.

ARCHAEOLOGICAL DISTRICT MUSEUM ★★★

Anastasi Sioukri & Vyroronos Str., near public Gardens   **Tel: 25 30 51 57**
Open: Tue-Fri 08-15.00 (Thur to 17.00)/ Sat: 09-15.00   Entrance Charge

Exhibits include finds from Amathus, Courion and other ancient places of Limassol district, from the Neolithic to the Roman periods, including pottery, jewellery coins, statues including a bust of Aphrodite.

FOLK ART MUSEUM ★★

253 Ayiou Andreou Street   **Tel: 25 36 23 03**   Open: Mon-Fri: 08.30-13.30 & 15-17.30 (Thur Jun-Sept 16-18.30)   Entrance Charge

Housed in restored 19th cent house it hosts an interesting collection of Cypriot Folk Art including national costumes, embroidery and tapestry.

MUNICIPAL ART GALLERY ★

103, 28th October Avenue, north of Municipal Gardens   **Tel: 25 58 62 12**
Open Mon-Fri: 07.30-13.45   Entrance Charge

A small but interesting collection of works of art, mainly by local contemporary artists, some well known.

TIME ELEVATOR ★★

In the old carob mill complex behind Medieval Castle.   **Tel: 25 76 28 28**
Open: May-Oct 10-20.00; Nov-Apr 09-18.00   Entrance Charge
www.timeelevatorcyprus.com

Travel through the ages of Cyprus History in a spectacular 4D pictorial experience
Also within the same premises: **Carob Museum** Entrance Free
Tel: 25 762828   Open Daily

medieval monuments

MEDIEVAL MUSEUM AND CASTLE ★★★

Richard and Berengaria Str., off Irinis Str, next to Old Harbour -

Tel:25 30 54 19 Open: Mon-Sat 09-17.00/ Sun 10-13.00   Entrance Charge

The only surviving medieval monument in town, originating from the Byzantine period. It was here in the small chapel that Richard the Lionheart married Berengaria in 1191 and made her Queen of England. It was strengthened by the Knights Templar and later by the Venetians. It was used by the Turks as a prison and by the British army as their headquarters during 2nd World War.

Visitors can explore the various halls and rooms, many of which exhibit various Medieval objects, including weapons, armoury and knight's uniforms, pottery and other objects covering the Medieval period.

Above Top:Medieval Castle of Limassol;
Left a Medieval Tombstone and above a Medieval
tray, both at the Museum

51

churches and religious places

There are a number of churches in the old town and along the sea promenade, none are of any ancient Byzantine or Medieval interest. They include:

Ayia Napa Cathedral, a massive structure dating to 1903; **Ayia Trias** dates to 1916; **Ayios Andronikos** by the sea front, built in Byzantine style in 1850 which contains very interesting icons. **St Barnabas Church**, open for Anglican services Tel: 25 36 27 13 and **St Catherine** *Catholic Church* open for Mass: 25 36 29 46

In the Old Quarter, close to the castle is the **Great Mosque** *(Djamir Kebir)*. It was built in the 16th cent on the foundations of an earlier Christian church. It is now in use.

Metropolitan Orthodox Church is **Panayia Catholiki**

Holy Bishopric of Limassol at Ayiou Andreou 306; Tel 25 86 43 00

For all religious places, entry is free when they are open, avoid times of services. (a donation is welcomed).

other places of interest

OLD HARBOUR / BOAT TRIPS

Once the main harbour for the town, it now shelters fishing boats and small pleasure boats. Boat Tours take visitors on coastal trips around the Akrotiri peninsular and as far as Pissouri Bay and Aphrodite's Birthplace further west.

Enjoy a short or long Boat Trip-Fishing trips can also be arranged.

There are a small number of tavernas and coffee shops by the entrance or near the old harbour.

PUBLIC GARDENS ★★

The pride of Limassol, the major green open space is a paradise for both Children and Adults. It hosts several annual festivities such as the *Flower Festival* in the Spring and the *Wine Festival* in early September, plus various activities related to Limassol's famous *Carnival* in late February - (movable).

For children: - **Playground** during daytime, free   **Zoo and Dinosaur Park**; **Tel: 25 58 83 45;** Open: daily 09-19.00 (Dinosaurs 10-19.00) Entrance Charge;

General:-**Open Air Theatre** - regular evening performances during summer months, mainly Free. *Gardens* are open daily during daylight. The public gardens provide facilities and cafeteria.

The shopping centre of Limassol or the village square are interesting to shoppers

shopping

Limassol is a good place for shopping. The tourist area offers many modern shops to satisfy most. But the real shopping is to be enjoyed in the Old Town of Limassol, where the old traditional shops sit next to modern boutiques some with designer label items. Starting from the seafront, work your way into Ayios Andreas Street and the surrounding areas plus the shopping centres.

* **Cyprus Handicraft Centre** - a foundation encouraging local crafts is at 25 Themidos Street   Tel: 25 30 51 18

For colourful Fresh Fruit and Vegetables there are two *Markets* at Genethlios Mitellas and Saripolos Street, close to the main Tourist Office.

swimming - water sports

Starting from the area opposite the Public Gardens and extending all the way to the top end of Limassol Bay, the beaches offer ideal spots for swimmers, in places with umbrellas and sunbeds. Note that all the beaches in front of the hotels are for everyone to use(hotel grounds and facilities are for their guests.)

Dhassoudi Beach, 5kms east of Limassol Town, is run and supervised by the tourist board and offers changing and other facilities. Tel: 25 32 28 11

All along the beaches there are organised and licensed centres offering a variety of exciting water sports.

Water sports and sandy beaches are an added attraction

EXCURSIONS

Akrotiri peninsula / classical route

Concentrated to the west of Limassol town are the most interesting places to explore and the *Aphrodite Route* which takes you to Aphrodite's Birthplace and Temple (see pages. 29) after exploring the ancient sites of Courion, see below.

FASSOURI PLANTATIONS ★/ LADY'S MILE BEACH ★★

South and west of Limassol are the agricultural areas of Citrus Groves. What makes the area interesting are the various plots which are protected from winds by enormous cypress trees lined up along both sides of roads creating an endless arch of shade.

On the eastern side, south of the port along the coast is the rather isolated and long stretch of sandy beach, **Lady's Mile.** Free from developments is usually empty and without facilities. Occasional winds make it ideal for windsurfing.

AKROTIRI / Salt lake / Old Church ★★

Further south, towards the Akrotiri Peninsula is the village of Akrotiri (beyond that the road is closed as it is the British Air Force base and military airport).

At the village, **Akrotiri Environmental Information Centre** provides valuable exhibits and photos related to the whole area.   **Tel 25 82 65 62** Entrance is free;   Open daily: Mon-Sun 08.30-15.00;

The **Salt Lake** to the east dominates the landscape and is a bird sanctuary, you may get a glimpse of Flamingos. It gets dry during summer months, but do not attempt to cross it.

Close by the, on the southern part of the Lake is the Convent of **Ayios Nikolaos of the Cats,** named so when it was founded around 325 AD as a monastery. Tel: **25 95 20 21** Cats were brought in by St Helena to destroy the growing population of snakes. It was used by the Franks as an estate and a chapel, then abandoned and now it is being restored and functions as a nunnery. Best reached from the Akrotiri village

Open during daylight- Admission is free (donation)

EPISKOPI GARRISON ★

This cannot be avoided by any visitor travelling along the old main road between Limassol and Paphos, entering just after the Temple of Apollo site. For security reasons, entry to the barracks and village is not allowed, but the twisted road running all the way to the valley with the cricket fields and out again is worth a drive. Here, traffic laws apply the same as those in the UK.

Bases Police Tel: 1443

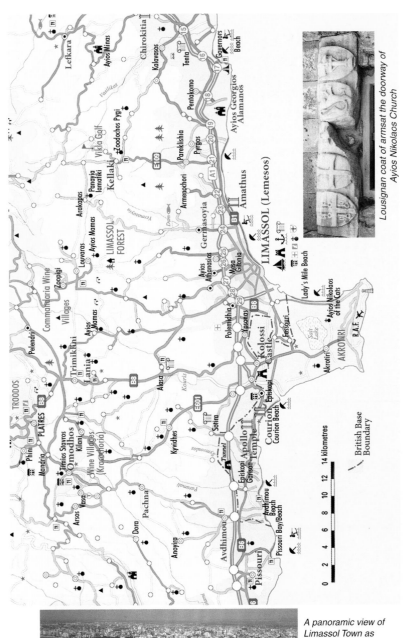

Lousignan coat of arms at the doorway of Ayios Nikolaos Church

A panoramic view of Limassol Town as seen from the air (CTO)

KOLOSSI CASTLE ★★★

14kms, 9miles, west of Limassol.   **Tel: 25 93 49 07**

Open: daily 08-17.00 (Jun-Aug to 19.30;/ Apr-May &Sep-Oct to 18.00)
Entrance Charge; Parking; Facilities

The most important Medieval Castle in the island, was the centre of the Grand Commanderie that ruled a wide area and benefited from wine making (famed for the sweet red wine of Commandaria which was consumed in Royal Courts of Europe and England), also for its rich sugar production.

It was controlled originally by the Order of St John of Jerusalem Knights and later by the Knights Templar. Originally built about 1210, the current structure dates to around 1454 and was successfully defended from Genoese attacks although damaged later by the Mameluke Arabs in 1425.

Despite the Turkish Ottoman occupation of the island in 1571, the Castle remained in control of the Venetian family till 1799, continuing sugar production which by then was declining. Restoration was started by the British administration in the 1930's.

It is one of the most popular monuments in the island.

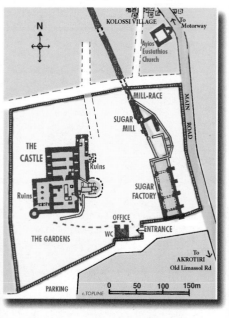

Above Left: A stamp featuring the Kolossi Castle;
Left: Lusignan coat of arms at the castle;
Above: Kolossi Castle site area map

56

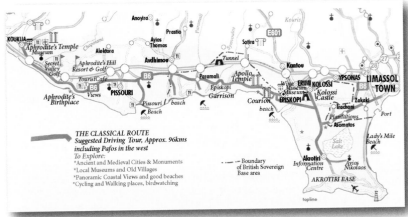

KOUKLIA
Aphrodite's Temple & Museum
Secret Valley Golf
Aphrodite's Hill Resort & Golf
TouristCafe
Aphrodite's Birthplace
PISSOURI
Views
Pissouri beach
Beach

Anoyira
Prastio
Ayios Thomas
Avdhimou
Paramali
Alektora

Sotira
E601
Tunnel
Apollo Temple
Episkopi Garrison
Courion beach

Kantou
Wine Museum
ERIMI KOLOSSI
EPISKOPI
Kolossi Castle

YPSONAS
LIMASSOL TOWN
Zakaki
Trachoni
Plantations
Asomatos
Salt Lake
Port
Lady's Mile Beach

Akrotiri Information Centre
Ayios Nikolaos
AKROTIRI BASE

THE CLASSICAL ROUTE
Suggested Driving Tour, Approx. 96kms
including Pafos in the west
To Explore:
*Ancient and Medieval Cities & Monuments
*Local Museums and Old Villages
*Panoramic Coastal Views and good beaches
*Cycling and Walking places, birdwatching

-- = Boundary
of British Sovereign
Base area

topline

*Above: View of
Kolossi Castle;
Left: A couple viewing
the ruins of the
Basilica*

57

ANCIENT CITY OF COURION (KOURION) ★★★

This is the most important monument of ancient Cyprus after Salamis which is in the occupied area of Famagusta. It is a site which is included in all Tours and most Cruise itineraries along the eastern Mediterranean.

19kms, 11miles west of Limassol, by the side of the old main road to Paphos.
Tel: 25 93 42 50

Open daily: Nov-Mar: 08-17.00 (Apr-May & Sep-Oct to 18.00/ Jun-Aug to19.30); Entrance Charge; Tourist Pavilion with Cafe, Facilities and shop on eastern side by the theatre.

History:- It was founded in the 14th-12th cent BC by Greek settlers and soon flourished, growing into a major Kingdom, controlling the rich valleys of the Couris river to the east below the cliffs. Its prosperity continued under the Romans and subsequently until the early years of Christianity.   A devastating earthquake destroyed the city around 365 AD. It was rebuilt but never reached its previous strength or glory.

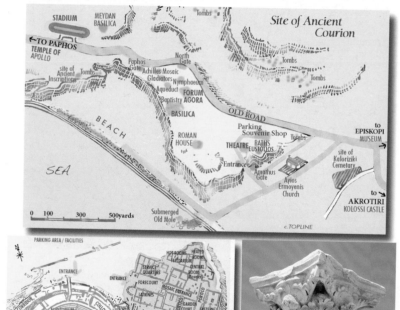

Above Top: *Location map of the Courion area;*
Above: *The Theatre and House of Eustolios plans;*
Right: *a column to be seen at Courion*

What to see at Courion:-

The Mosaics - Most are to be found in the various houses on the western side of the area such as those of *Achilles* and the *Gladiators*. Other floor mosaics are in the **House of Eustolios** - a Roman villa, to the east of the theatre and include the well known *Creation*.

Roman Forum and the **Stoa** date to the 2nd century AD

Early Christian Basilica - This was built on the foundations of an earlier temple in a commanding position overlooking the sea, an impressive and massive structure, it dates to the 5th century AD.

The Theatre, an impressive Greco-Roman theatre restored in the early 1960's dating from the Hellenistic times and widely used by the Romans, finally abandoned by the Christian new order.   It is the most visited of all the parts of the city. Concerts and theatrical productions are performed there during the summer months. Most important is the annual Courion Drama Festival. The highlights are ancient Greek Drama, Shakespeare plays and quality musical shows (dates and information from the Tourist Offices).

The Public Baths - a sophisticated structure on the northern part of the **Eustolios House**, with firing chamber clearly visible and well preserved.

Roman House - This unearthed fascinating discoveries which have been studied by American Archaeologists. The finds include some undisturbed human remains of victims of the great earthquake of July in 365 AD. In addition, tools, artifacts and other objects remained unharmed where they fell.

General View of Courion Ancient Theatre

59

Above: General view of the Basilica and the coastline beyond;
Below: A view of columns from the southern building of Apollo Temple

Outside the City, along the road to the Temple are the remains of the once active **Stadium** used for athletic and general sporting events up to the 4th cent AD and seating around 6,000.

COURION MUSEUM ★★

This is to be found at Episkopi Village, to the east of the ancient city, some 14kms, 9miles west of Limassol   **Tel: 25 93 24 53**

Open:Mon-Fri 09-14.00 (Thu to17.00) Entrance Charge

It contains various artifacts including pottery, coins, oil-lamps, sculptures and very important, the three skeletons of the family found at the Roman House, victims of the earthquake.

Mosaic floor from the House
of Eustolios

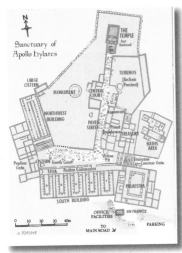

Left: The sanctuary of the Temple of Apollo plan
Above: A view of the Temple of Apollo and area

SANCTUARY OF APOLLO HYLATES (God of the Woods) ★★★

3kms west of Courion, off the main road, well sign posted   Tel: 25 99 10 49

Open daily; Nov-Mar 08-17.00 (Apr-May & Sep-Oct to 18.00/ Jun-Aug to
19.30)   Entrance Charge; Parking; Facilities

An important Temple, partially restored that covers a wide area. It was a
sacred place for over 1,200 years, from around 800 BC to 400 AD It was
dedicated to the god Apollo, protector of the woods and forest, amongst
other things,

To be seen around the site are:-

The Temple, the sacred place of worship.

The Archaic Precinct, close to the Temple including the Priest's House and the
Treasury.

Accommodation Buildings on the northern and southern areas to house
visitors to the Temple.

The Palaestra, was the recreation area entertaining visitors.

The Baths, the well organised complex include changing rooms and the
graduated stages of rooms providing water from cold to steam.

61

the Wine Villages (ta krasochoria)

In the northwestern areas of Limassol, under the shadow of the southern foothills of the Troodos mountains are to be explored the numerous grape growing villages - grapes are collected at the end of August for the wine making - some find their way to the major wineries in Limassol, others are turned into wine at the local wineries located in some of the listed villages and visitors are welcomed.

OMODHOS ★★★

11kms south of Platres is a major centre and a friendly village with a welcoming paved square. It has retained many of its old traditional products which are to be found in the numerous shops.

The Monastery of Stavros (The Holy Cross) is impressive. The old monastic buildings surround the church which contains numerous icons and a golden cross. It is open during daylight, free (donations welcomed) and it celebrates on September 14th with a feast.

Traditional Winery Press - Open daily during daytime Entrance free

-5- Olympus Winery/ Omodhos: Tel: 25 57 33 91

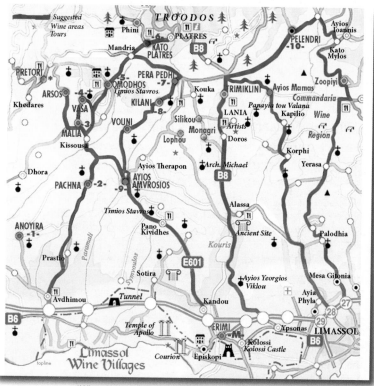

*Winery is in the Paphos district

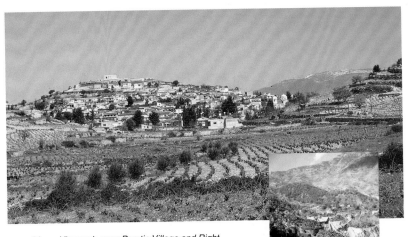

Above: Vineyards near Prastio Village and Right, collection of the grapes for the wine making

KILANI ★★

An attractive village which has preserved much of its architectural heritage, with its narrow streets. It is in the centre of the wine growing areas. Within the village is the ***Ecclesiastical Museum*** exhibiting religious objects and books. **Tel: 99 60 81 96;** Open during daylight, it is free. Next to it is the Viticultural Museum.

Outside the village is the church of **Ayia Mavra** which is well known to locals.

-8- Kilani Wineries/ Vlasidis: 99 44 15 74 / **Ayia Mavri:**
Tel: 25 47 02 25

ARSOS VILLAGE ★★

Folk Art Museum private collection - Tel: 25 94 32 23 by appointment - Entrance Charge

VASSA VILLAGE ★★

A medieval village with many traditional old buildings including the preserved house of the well known Cypriot poet, Lipertis. A centre of wine production, also famed for its mineral water. A small **Ecclesiastical Museum** exhibits religious objects and is open daily. -

-4- Vassa Winery/ Vassa: Tel: 25 94 58 88 ; Tel: 25 94 59 99

ANOYIRA VILLAGE ★

A village with long history and restored old houses. It has an unusual **Museum of Pastelli**, grape by-products for various uses: **Tel: 25 22 23 57** - by appointment

Also here you get the chance to see how Olive Oil is made at the working mill of **Oleasto Museum** - *the house of olive....* Tel: **99 52 50 93** which is open daily 10-19.00

-1- Domaine Nicolaides Winery/ Anoyira: Tel: 25 22 17 09

63

AYIOS AMVROSIOS ★★

Here we see the "first" *Ecological Winery* in the island which is open to visitors Mon-Fri 08-14.00 and is worth a visit.   Tel: 25 24 3981

-9- Ecological Winery/ Ayios Amvrosios: Tel: 25 94 39 81

ERIMI VILLAGE ★★

Further south close to the motorway, this ancient village houses the **-M- Cyprus Wine Museum,** of the region, including the history of wine making in the island with pots, other antiquities and materials. Situated at 42 Paphos Street, **Tel: 25 87 38 08**   Open: Daily 09-17.00 Entrance Charge.   email:cypruswinemuseum@cytanet.com.cy

other wineries of the area plus Telephone numbers:
- **-2- at Pachna: Yiaskouris:** 99 63 37 30/ **Monolithos**: 99 16 59 95
- **-3- Ktima Winery/ Malia Village:** 25 85 31 00
- **-7- Constantinou Winery/ Pera Pedhi:** 25 47 03 70
- **-6- Lambouri Winery/ Kato Platres:** 99 44 00 48

Above Left: Monastery of Stavros courtyard at Omodhos (CTO); Above Right: A craft shop at Omodhos Square; Below: The picturesque village of of Lophou, west of Monagri, in the heart of the wine village region (CTO)

the commandaria wine region

North of Limassol, on the southeastern slopes of Troodos are the areas which mainly produce the *Commandaria* type of sweet desert wine. It was a popular medieval wine and takes its name from *Commanderie*. This type of wine is also produced in some parts of southern Europe.

ZOOPYGI ★★

A picturesque village surrounded by vineyards, a major centre of Commandaria wine but also for making the traditional local spirit called Zivania which recently has become very popular for its "cures".

LANIA VILLAGE ★★★

A beautiful village with traditional houses off the main road from Limassol to Platres. It has now become a favourite place for artists both local and British. Some have set up their own studios and galleries here. It is a place highly recommended to visitors to stroll in the old narrow streets and rest by the village taverna/cafe.

The Village of the Artists, take your own sketchbook and join them.....

LOUVARAS ★

26 kms from Limassol. Commanding excellent views, this was a medieval village and has an interesting medieval church of *Ayios Mamas* with numerous wall paintings. Request the key from the local priest. Call Tel: **25 54 21 42** or mob: **99 31 88 32**.

Other Commandaria region villages such as **Pelendri, Agros** and **Palechori,** are listed in the Pitsilia district of the Troodos Mountains section.

-10-Tsiakkas Winery/ Pelendri: Tel: 99 56 78 98 ; Tel: 25 99 10 80
tsiakkas@logosnet.cy.net

An artists studio at Lania village, most usually open to the pubic at weekends

65

east of Limassol and the bay

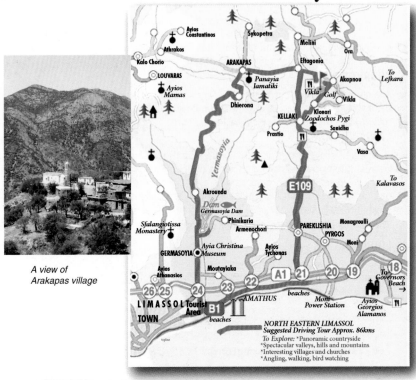

A view of Arakapas village

GERMASOYIA ★★★

The village right to the north of the Germasoyia Tourist area of Limassol. the village centre has retained its old traditional atmosphere and narrow streets. The church of *Ayia Christina* houses a small **religious museum: Tel: 25 87 98 98**

KELLAKI VILLAGE / Arakapas Village / Churches ★★

These inland areas north east of Limassol are mainly isolated and reward travellers with their beauty and the peacefulness of their surroundings.

Kellaki, known for its Commandaria wine has an interesting and well known church of **Zoodochos Pygi**. To visit the church call Tel; 25 62 20 17. It contains good icons.

Arakapas further north is more isolated. It is known for the church of **Panayia Iamatiki,** now a Convent. The church is of Latin origin with Byzantine influence which is reflected in the numerous wall paintings.

Vikla Golf - 20kms north of Limassol, near Kellaki village - 18 holes-par 72-5200meters   **Tel: 25 62 28 94**   Ideal surroundings for a day out to explore and relax. Taverna   email: viklagolf@cytanet.com.cy

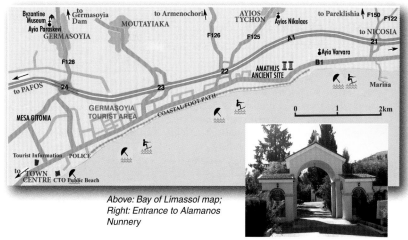

Above: Bay of Limassol map;
Right: Entrance to Alamanos
Nunnery

THE BAY OF LIMASSOL / Beaches / Marina ★★

The whole Bay is dotted with hotels all along the coast and they provide numerous areas for swimming which are open to the public.

St Raphael private Marina in front of the hotel is one of the best equipped in the Eastern Mediterranean.

Tel: 25 63 61 00 em-raphael@spidernet.com.cy

AYIOS GEORGIOS ALAMANOU CONVENT ★★

19kms east of Limassol   **Tel 25 63 23 29**

To the south of the motorway - exit18 this expanding nunnery is situated in peaceful surroundings close to the sea. By the entrance, the church is open to the public, the monastic buildings are private. Drive further down the narrow road to the pebble beach to see interesting white chalk rock formations.

GOVERNORS BEACH ★★★

This is further east, exit 17 from the motorway, a popular beach with some facilities and coffee shops. A regular bus service connects the beach with Limassol Town (Old Harbour) during the summer.

Ayios Georgios Alamanou coast, a short drive from the monastery. The Bay of Limassol is visible in the distance

67

AMATHUS ANCIENT CITY ★★★

11kms, 7miles east of Limassol town centre, along the Bay

Open: Nov-Mar 09-17.00 (Apr-May & Sep-Oct to18.00/ Jun-Aug to19.30)
Entrance Charge;   Limited Parking

The Ancient Kingdom of Amathus was one of the most important in the island. One theory is that it was founded by Greek settlers, the other by Phoenician traders. One thing is for sure, the Kingdom had a mixed and cosmopolitan culture including Jewish and Egyptian people. It prospered for many hundreds of years in antiquity.

This affluence continued under the Romans and it was one of the four capital districts. Its decline started in the early part of the Byzantine period due to numerous devastating Arab raids.

By the time Richard the Lionheart landed here in 1191 its importance as a city had declined to nothing. Over the following centuries, stones and other material were re-used in other places - to build in Larnaca in medieval times for instance. It was even transported to Egypt to build the Suez Canal, and the notorious Cesnola, who excavated without care, transported finds from here to the New York Metropolitan Museum.

Partially excavated Amathus, some of what has survived includes;

The Akropolis - high at the top commanding panoramic views.

Early Christian Basilica - by the Akropolis, was built on the site of the Temple of Aphrodite. It is worth climbing up the hill to the top.

Basilica - remains of which are to be seen by the road side next to the entrance.

Lower City and Agora, are the main ruins to have been excavated and **collonades have been restored.**

The Harbour- this is now submerged under sea water by the edge of the road. It can be seen on a very clear and calm day.

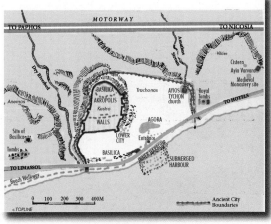

Above: A stamp showing the the Lion of Amathus on a coin;
Left: Site plan of the ancient city

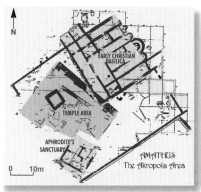

Above: Plan of the Amathus Akropolis;   Above Right: A colossal limestone jar was found
here , dating to the 6th cent BC. It was moved to the Louvre in Paris;
Below: Columns of the Agora at the ancient site. The Akropolis is seen in the background

useful telephones

Transport Services........25 35 40 50
Intercity Buses................24 64 34 92
Urban Buses.....................25 37 05 92
Taxi Services...................25 36 41 14
Express 25 87 76 66
Chemists-24hr service 90 90 14 05
First Aid.................. ....25 30 57 70
Old Hospital................ .....25 30 53 33
New General Hospital 25 80 11 00
Private Doctors Care..90 90 14 25

Police Headquartes..... ..25 80 50 50
Local Administration....25 36 25 03
Post Office, main.......... ..25 80 22 59
Antiquities...........................25 36 63 32
Nautical Club................ ..25 32 42 82
Customs............................25 36 52 95
Port Information.............25 81 92 00

St Raphael Marina....... ..25 63 61 00
Central Library............. ...25 36 21 55
Fire Service........................25 80 54 00
Electricity............................25 84 90 00
Water Authority......... ....25 36 27 56
Police/Fire/Ambulance 112 or 199
Forest Fires......................1407
British Bases Police........1443
Avdhimou Health 25 22 13 06
Lania Health Care........ 25 43 24 48
Omodhos Hospital......25 42 12 54
Religious Services
Anglican Church.......... ....25 36 27 13
Catholic Mass..................25 36 29 46
Armenia Church.............24 65 44 35
Greek Evangelical...........25 38 27 18
German Evangelical..... ..25 31 70 92
Coptic Orthodox..........99 61 57 93
Russian Orthodox........25 33 36 18

distances
Distance from Limassol to:

	kms	miles
Nicosia........................	86	54
Paphos............................	68	42
Polis.............................	98	61
Larnaka......................	71	44
Ayia Napa..................	106	66
Paralimni....................	110	68
Troodos......................	45	28
Larnaka Airport.........	70	44
Paphos Airport..............	60	36

Panoramic view of Kellaki village (Kleanthis Kotsiofides)

The private Marina at St Raphael – Limassol town in the distance;

activities

Watermania - Fassouri area, near Trahoni, west of Limassol-   Tel: 25 71 42 35
email: fasouriwatermania@cytanet.com.cy   www.fasouri-watermania.com
Open: daily: May - Oct   Entrance Charge Parking; Catering; Facilities

Donkey Sanctuary - Vouni village -36kms north of Limassol. Tel: 25 94 54 88
email: cyprusdonkey@cheerful.com   web: www.donkeycyprus.com
Open: Mon - Sat: 10-16.00   Entrance Charge Parking; Cafe

Reptile House - for all the Family   Old Port Area, by entrance square
Tel: 25 37 27 79 / 99 43 75 15   Open: Daily   Entrance Charge

Municipal Park -ideal for children with playing ground, zoo and other facilities.

Wild Valley Ostrich Farm; Pissouri - Plataniskia Road   Tel: 25 99 10 10
www.ostrich.com.cy

Elias Beach County Club Tel: 25 63 60 00 Sports Centre incl. tennis; football;
shooting; archery; horse riding; golf Entrance Charge. *Check for availability*

Vikla Golf - 20kms north of Limassol, near Kellaki village - 18 holes-par 72-
5200meters   Tel: 25 62 28 94   Ideal surroundings for a day out to explore
and relax. Taverna   email: viklagolf@cytanet.com.cy

Amathus Riding Centre Pareklishia village, off the motorway-northern area of
Limassol   Tel: 25 60 41 09/99 60 41 09

Curium Equestrian Centre, Courium Beach   Tel: 99 56 42 32 & 99 76 72 18

*Above Right: A Courion Theatre
performance; Above; Omodhos village
street; Right: The carnival parade, the
most colourful event in Limassol(CTO)*

71

Larnaka(Larnaca)
old glories new strengths

Larnaka Marina and its Promenade (CTO)

Being established in ancient times by the adventurous and commercially orientated Phoenicians, the new town is built virtually on top of the ancient city of Kition.

It went through Hellenistic Greek, Roman and Byzantine stages and suffered much from Arab raids. There was a recovery during the Lusignan and Genoese period in Medieval times but it was during the 18 -19th centuries that European traders started to revitalise Larnaka, also known as Larnic.

With the establishment of an International Airport in the late 1970's the town is now experiencing continuous growth and expansion. It offers good shopping, monuments within the city and the countryside, long sandy beaches on the northern parts of the Bay, a unique Palm Tree Promenade and an international Marina.

An ideal place to visit, to explore and to enjoy.

LARNAKA TOP ATTRACTIONS

Larnaka Town Walking Tours

a- It is easy in Larnaka to organise your own walk. A round trip from the Promenade to the Medieval Fort, inland to majestic Ayios Lazarus church, up to the old town and shopping centre, to the Pierides Collection and further on to the site of Ancient Kition.

Arrange it as you wish at your own pace or:

b- Join an organised guided walking tour with the Tourist Office:
    Tel 24 65 43 22 -   This Offers:
1) - Past and Present Larnaka.
2) - Scala and the Craft Shops through the old town starting at the fort.

Beach Walk

Not so much a beach walk but a stroll along the coast, starting from the Marina, heading south along the Palm Tree Promenade, past the Medieval Fort, along the coastal road towards the fishing harbour and McKenzie Beach overlooking the airport.

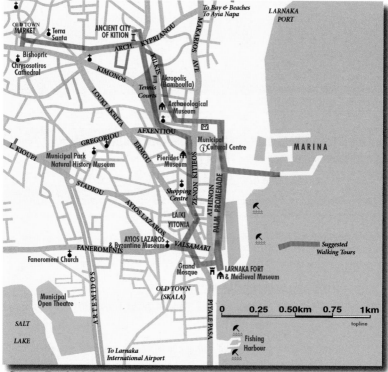

Cyprus Tourist Information Offices
Main Office: Vasileos Pavlou Square Tel: 24 65 43 22
Larnaka Airport: Tel: 24 64 35 76 (daily to 23.00)

73

what to see and what to do
museums and galleries / collections

LARNAKA FORT - Medieval Museum ★★★
By the Sea Front **Tel: 24 30 45 76**

Open: Mon-Fri: 09-17.00 (Nov-May & Sep-Oct) /
Jun-Aug to19.30 .   Entrance Charge; Facilities

This small collection of Larnaka's Medieval History is worth visiting together
with a tour of the Fort (see other section). It contains weapons, pottery and
photographs plus other relevant information.

BYZANTINE ECCLESIASTICAL MUSEUM ★★★
Next to Ayios Lazarus Church **Tel: 24 65 24 98**

Open: Mon-Sat: 08.30-12.30 & 15-17.30 (Wed & Sat up to 12.30)
Entrance Charge

The Museum is small but very interesting for the excellent presentation and
artistic value of the numerous icons, the quality of manuscripts and Bibles and
the various ecclesiastical ornaments and objects.

PIERIDES ARCHAEOLOGICAL MUSEUM AND FOUNDATION ★★
4 Zenonos Kitieos Street   **Tel: 24 81 45 55**

Open: Mon-Thurs. 09-16.00/ Fri-Sat 09-13.00   Entrance Charge

A private collection housed in a preserved old house, founded by Demetrios
Pierides (1811-1895) and continued by his family.

On display is a large assemblage of pottery, vases, statuettes, terracotta,
glassware and jewellery.

DISTRICT ARCHAEOLOGICAL MUSEUM ★★
 Kalogreon Square, near tennis court **Tel: 24 30 41 69**

Open: Tue-Fri 08-15.00 (Thurs to17.00)/ Sat: 09-15.00   Entrance Charge

The museum exhibits many of the finds from the ancient site of Kition,
Chirokitia, the Tekke site and other places.

It includes pottery, vases, statues, tomb stones and others covering all periods
up to the Romans.

Above Top: Europa Square next to the Municipal Cultural Centre and the Palm Tree Promenade further south; Above:Clay bulls at the Pierides Museum, c1300bc;
Right: The bust of Kimon (see page 79) at the Palm Tree Promenade

MUNICIPAL CULTURAL CENTRE ★★ Paleontology Museum / Gallery

In the Old Customs House - Municipal Cultural Centre, opposite the Marina, Europa Platia (Square).

Paleontology Collection (Pierides Tornarides) **Tel 24 62 85 87**

Open: Tue-Fri 09-14.00/ Sat-Sun 09-12.00 (Sun close Jun-Aug) - Entrance Free - Including a fossil collection

Municipal Gallery   Tel: 24 65 88 48   Open: Mon-Fri: 09-16.00 Sat: 10-13.00   Entrance Free;   Long exhibitions by local Artists.

NATURAL HISTORY MUSEUM ★★

Within the Municipal Gardens , Gregoriou Afxentiou Ave. **Tel: 24 65 25 69**
Open: Mon-Fri: 09-16.00 / Sat: 10-13.00 Entrance Charge

ancient sites and monuments

ANCIENT CITY OF KITION ★★★

Just off Leontios Macheras Street, about 500m from the Museum; Entrance Charge Open: Mon-Fri 08-14.30 (Thurs to 15.00) No Facilities.

Believed to be one of the oldest cities in the world reputed to have been founded by one of Noah's grandsons named "Kittim" which was mentioned in the old Testament.

The Phoenicians established a commercial centre around the 9th cent. BC, although finds show that the Mycenean Greeks came before at around 1400-1100BC. Great wealth was created from the inland Copper mines of Tamassos and then traded and exported by the Phoenicians.

It was an ally of the Persians during their control of the island and various battles took place, including attempts from the mainland Greek Navy to liberate it. Ruins to be seen include gigantic wall structures and parts of the Temple.

Around the area are lesser remains preserved in street corners and *The Akropolis*, know as **Bamboulla Hill,** on the northern part of the museum area. They can be viewed from the road or the park.

Above: Gold coin of the Kition King Pumiathon (361-312 BC); Left: Part of the excavated site; Bottom Left: Site plan map; Below: Aerial view of the Temple and site, from the Cyprus Museum

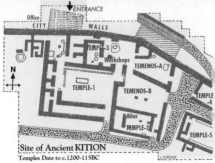

Site of Ancient KITION
Temples Date to c.1200-115BC

Two views of The Medieval Fort of Larnaka.
According to a European traveller in 1799, any Christian ships due to dock in Larnaka had to wait out at sea for 3-4 days so that a messenger could go to Nicosia to obtain permission to stay, otherwise they had to sail on.......

LARNAKA FORT ★★★ *- also see under museums*

On the Seafront; **Tel 24 30 45 76**; Entrance Charge

It was used around 1625 by the Ottoman Turks for the defence of the town,, mainly from Pirates, and used most of the time as a prison.

The British also used the fort as a prison, barracks for the garrison and as police headquarters.

As well as a museum it is also used for cultural activities mainly in the summer.

churches / places of worship

TERRA SANTA CATHOLIC CHURCH ★

Tel: 24 64 28 58   Dedicated to Santa Maria della Gratia

CATHEDRAL OF AYIOS CHRYSOSOTIROS ★

The Metropolitan Cathedral dating to around 1853 but contains a much older iconostasi with interesting icons.

GRAND MOSQUE (Cami Kebir) ★

Situated opposite the Fort; Open during daylight; Entrance Free (donation). Used for regular prayers. Originally it was the Latin church of St Katherine, later converted into a mosque. Outside it has an old fountain by the road.

METROPOLITAN CHURCH of Soteros Holy Bishopric of Kition, Metropoleos Square   Tel: 24 65 22 69

77

Above: The church of Ayios Lazarus - the Byzantine museum is behind the church;
Right: The icon of the Virgin and the child at the church;
Left: Tomb at the rear, where consuls and merchants were buried in 17th & 18th cent.

AYIOS LAZARUS CHURCH ★★★

Ayios Lazarus Square, few minutes walk from the Fort.   **Tel: 24 65 24 98**
Entrance to church Free (donation)   Open: Mon-Sun Apr-Aug 08-12.30
& 14.30-18.30 (Sep-Mar afternoons14.40-17.30)

A very important church, originally dates to around 900BC built by Byzantine
Emperor Leo VI on the site where St Lazarus was buried.

The present church is of the 17th century, the bell tower more recent and it
is the major exterior attraction. The interior presents a rich Byzantine atmosphere with priceless icons and a gilded iconostasi. Beneath the church you can
still see the tomb and shrine of the saint.

PHANEROMENI CHURCH ★

Phaneromenis Avenue; Open during daylight; Entrance Free (donation)

A modern church but contains an ancient rock chamber, a Roman tomb which
is preserved.

other places of interest

LAIKI YITONIA ★★

Behind the seafront of Palm Tree Promenade and north of the Fort. Restored parts of old Larnaka offer shopping for arts and crafts, other souvenir shops and tavernas, ideal to walk around.

PALM TREE PROMENADE (Finikoudhes) ★★★

The pride of Larnaka - A palm tree promenade, on the eastern side is the beach and the sea, opposite a line of shops, cafeterias and restaurants. A lovely place for everyone to sit and enjoy watching the world go by. **Bust of Kimon:** Kimon was a naval commander who died during a sea battle to Liberate the Kingdom City from the Persian rule. His bust stands along the Palm Tree Promenade.

THE AQUEDUCT (Kamares) ★★

On the western outskirts of Larnaka, along the road to Limassol. Around 30 dominant arches remain which were once part of the aqueduct built in the 18th century to bring water from the Troodos mountains to Larnaka.

MUNICIPAL PARK ★★

A welcoming small green triangle by Gregorios Afxentiou Avenue; Open during daylight; Entrance Free. Here is situated the Museum of Natural History (see under museums). It is an interesting place for children and adults alike. The Town's Municipal Library is also situated here.

Outside by the roundabout is the bust of the famous philosopher **ZENO KITIEUS (Zeno of Kition),** founder of the Stoic Philosophy. He was born in Larnaka c335BC but spent most of his time in Athens teaching.

LARNAKA MARINA ★★

Tel: 24 65 31 10 email: larnaca.marina@cytanet.com.cy The first of its kind in Cyprus, this is situated on the northern end of the Palm Tree Promenade. It has facilities for over 450 yachts of various sizes. You can walk along the southern pier and admire the boats.

FISHING HARBOUR ★★

To the south of the port towards the McKenzie area. This is a small picturesque harbour mainly for fishing boats but also small boats offering Boat Trips along the coast. It is surrounded by a few fish restaurants.

Left: Fishing harbour of McKenzie; Right: The famous philosopher Zeno on a stamp

79

Left: Part of the market in old Larnaka area; Right: A traditional artisans shop in the area

shopping

The modern shopping area of Larnaka is concentrated along the eastern side of Gregorios Afxentiou Avenue and surrounding streets. Kimonos Avenue and the areas behind the Promenade are the heart of old Larnaka and offer a variety of shops, including the restored Laiki Yitonia

Also worth visiting is the small Fruit Market in the old quarter at Ermou Street.

* **Cyprus Handicraft Centre** - a foundation for local crafts and arts: 6 Cosma Lysioti Street Tel: 24 30 43 27

swimming - water sports

A small beach in front of the Palm Tree Promenade provides umbrellas and beds (chargeable); Further south is MacKenzie Beach, just to the north of the airport which is also known for its numerous tavernas.

The main beaches and the water sport activities are to be found further north, a few kms drive along the bay of Larnaka

The golden Sands of the Bay of Larnaka are popular for both bathers and sea sports

EXCURSIONS
south and west Larnaka

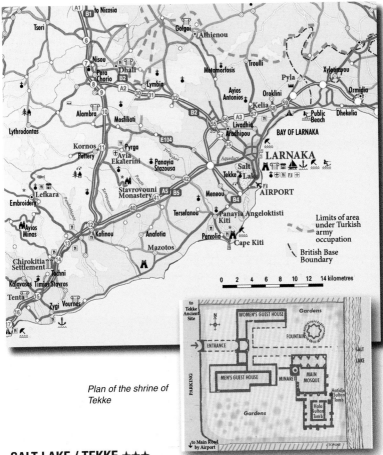

Plan of the shrine of Tekke

SALT LAKE / TEKKE ★★★

A phenomenon situated just to the west of Larnaka Airport, the lake gets its sea water from underground passages. It evaporates in the summer months and leaves layers of sea salt which in the old days was a valuable commodity.

A popular and large lake visited by migrating birds, most famous being the red flamingos.

One can not miss the high pointed mountain peak in the far distance to the west, that of Stavrovouni Monastery.

81

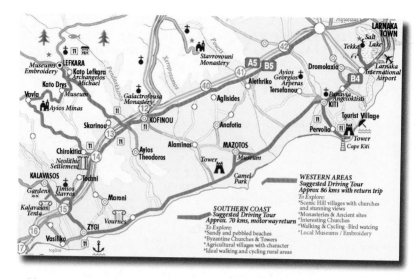

Nearer, amongst palm trees is the **Tekke Shrine - Hala Sultan -** 5kms south of Larnaka

A road on the southern part of the lake (off the main road) takes you to the entrance. It is open Daily: Jun-Aug 08-19.30/ Apr-May & Sep-Oct 08-18.00/ (Nov-Mar 08-17.00);   Entrance Free (donation). Parking.

It is one of the most important Moslem Shrines and contains the *Tomb of Umm Haram*, an aunt of the Prophet Mohammed, who lost her life falling from her horse whilst on a visit to Cyprus. As this is a religious site, visitors are requested to dress modestly and respect the shrine.

The Salt Lake and the Tekke are surrounded by palms. In the distance is the prominent Mountain of the Cross, (Stavrovouni)

PANAYIA ANGELOKTISTI ★★★

This church - built by the Angels - is situated in Kiti village, 10kms to the south of Larnaka. Tel: **24 42 46 46**
Open: Mon-Sun 08-12.00 & 14-16.00 (Jun-Aug to 18.00)   Entrance Free (donations) Respectable dress code; Parking area opposite

An important, impressive medieval structure built on the foundations of an early 5th century church. It contains excellent icons and one of the oldest mosaic walls in the island, that of Virgin Mary, believed to be of the 6th century.

Adjoining the church is the *Latin Chapel* which was added in the 13-14th centuries and contains several icons of the Italian style.

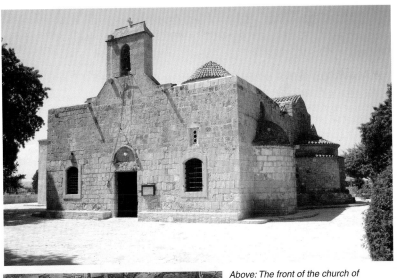

Above: The front of the church of Panayia Angeloktisti;
Left: The impressive 6th cent mosaic wall of the Virgin and Child;
Below: The Venetian Watch Tower (see next page)

CAPE KITI / Tower / Beach ★★

An expanding tourist area around **Pervola** and the Faros area of the Old Light House. The beach nearby provides good sand and some water sports.

The Medieval **Venetian Tower** has been restored, it was part of an extensive 'look out' system to keep watch for the threat posed by the Ottoman Turks. The Tower is closed to the public.

MAZOTOS VILLAGE / Sculpture Museum ★★

This **Naive Sculpture Museum** is the creation of sculptor and artist Costas Argyrou;   Tel: **24 99 16 33**
Open: Tue-Sat 09-12.00 & 14-16.00/ Sun 09-14.00   Entrance Charge

ZYGI VILLAGE ★★

Further south along the coast towards Limassol is this small fishing village, celebrated mainly by locals for its numerous fish tavernas by the small wooden pier.

KALAVASOS TENTA SITE / Village / Herb Garden ★★

40kms west of Larnaka, 2.5kms from motorway exit 15   Kalavasos village is old and in ancient times a centre for mining iron pyrates and gypsum (transported by rail to Zygi for export.) The village is picturesque with narrow streets and old restored houses. There are plans to establish a small railway line connecting the ancient site, the village and the ancient copper mines, where a museum is also planned.

Kalavasos Tenta ancient Neolithic site with some parts preserved and covered with a roof. Open: Mon-Fri: Nov -Mar 08.30-16.00/ Apr-Oct: 09.30-17.00 Entrance Charge; Parking
Aromatic Herb Garden - unusual and interesting to lovers of herbs.
Tel 99 53 54 60   Open: Mon-Sat 09.30-12.00 & 15-18.00

Above Left: The old train from the mines of Kalavasos has been preserved as a museum; Left: General view of Kalavasos Tenta before it was covered; Above: The popular village of Tochni, between Kalavasos and Chirokitia.

CHIROKITIA ANCIENT NEOLITHIC SETTLEMENT ★★★

Exit 14 of the motorway; 48kms from Nicosia, 38kms from Larnaka

Tel: 24 32 27 10   Open daily: Nov-Mar 08-17.00 (Apr-May & Sep-Oct to 18.00/ Jun-Aug to 19.30) Entrance Charge;   Parking;
Tavernas by motorway exit

One of the oldest settlements in Cyprus dating to around 6,800BC and one of the most important in the whole of the Eastern Mediterranean.

First excavated in 1934 it has revealed a wealth of information about the life, customs and day to day living in those far away times. Most dramatic were the finds of bodies buried in various layers under the floors of dwellings.

Many of the finds are on display at the Cyprus Museum in Nicosia. Next to the main entrance, five dwellings have been reconstructed, based on excavated findings.

Left: Reconstructed dwellings at Chirokitia site; Below: Part of the ancient settlement with its preserved ancient houses. Bottom: Site plan of the excavated area of Chirokitia

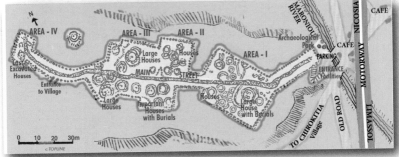

LEFKARA VILLAGE / Embroidery ★★★

40kms west of Larnaka, 8kms west from exit 13 of motorway.

A village that resembles an Italian or Spanish village dating from its medieval period. It is most famous as the centre of the celebrated Embroidery Lace which has been the main occupation of the villagers for centuries.

Patterns are mainly geometric with diamond zig-zag lines, but other motifs such as crosses, butterflies and florals are also used. Standards of work are extremely high and include bed covers, sheets, table clothes, pillow cases.

The village itself is welcoming, if you drive through be aware of narrow streets, and enjoy the numerous shops selling the local merchandise which in addition to Lace includes silverware, jewellery and the famous sweet, Lokoumia. To visit at the village:

Lefkara Embroidery Museum (Patsalos residence); Including Silverware and Lace: **Tel: 24 34 23 26**
Open: Mon-Thu 09.30-16.00/ Fri & Sat 10-16.00; Entrance Charge

Fatsa Wax Museum, depicting scenes from daily activities and rural life.
Tel: 24 62 10 48 Open Daily: Nov-Apr 09-17.30 (May-Oct to19.00)
Entrance Charge - concessions

Archangelos Michael Chapel, is a 12th century Byzantine chapel which contains good wall paintings and is situated at the edge of Kato Lefkara surrounded by the natural beauty.

AYIOS MINAS CONVENT/ KATO DRYS ★★

Near the village of Kato Drys **Tel: 24 34 29 52** Open Daily: May-Sep 08-12.00 & 15-18.00/ Oct-Apr & 14-17.00. Groups welcomed by appointment Entrance Free (donation); Dress code

This tranquil religious retreat of nuns is surrounded by picturesque country-side. Honey production and Icon painting are the major products of the nuns. They are usually for sale in a shop outside the convent.

Rural Museum at **Kato Drys** village. Established and run by the Papachristou family; **Tel: 24 34 26 48** Open: Mon-Fri 09-14.00; Small Entrance Charge

The Nunnery of Ayios Minas, a place of interest to visit

Above: A general view of Lefkara village. Dominant is the church of the Holy Cross; Left: Lefkaritica Lace, the well known embroidery, an industry with roots in the middle ages, including pillow cases, mats, table clothes, bed covers....

Above and Left: Streets of Lefkara with their traditional shops selling the famous embroidery lace, silver-ware, gold objects...

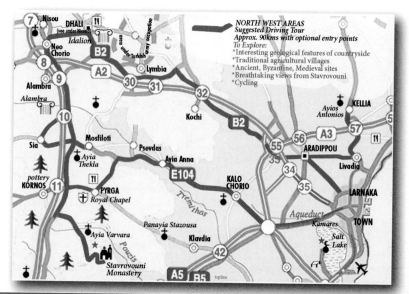

The impressive Monastery of Stavrovouni, the Mountain of the Cross, situated right at the top providing breathtaking views

west central and northern areas

STAVROVOUNI MONASTERY (Mountain of the Cross) ★★★

40kms west of Larnaka; 9kms from the Nicosia motorway, exit 11;
Tel: 24 53 36 30 (automatic dial) Driving to the top needs care round
bends; Parking at top by square. Bookshop and facilities.

Entrance to monastic area only to men, if properly dressed; Sep-Mar 08-12.00 &14-17.00/ Apr-Aug 08-12.00 & 15-18.00; Entrance Free(donations)
Women may visit the Sunday service in the church.

It is worth just the drive to the top and to wander around the square. The
views from the top are breathtaking in all directions and Larnaka town and
coastline is visible in the distance.

It is believed that a Temple of Aphrodite once stood at the summit where the
present day monastery is. This was originally established in 325AD by Saint
Helena, mother of the first Christian Emperor Constantine on her return from
the Holy Land when she stopped in the island and came here. Parts of relics
from the Holy Cross that she carried with her were left here.

In medieval times it was under the control of the Latin church and during the
Ottoman rule suffered various calamities from earthquakes, fires and raids. It
was then abandoned until the 17th century when it was re-build by Orthodox monks.

The brotherhood of Orthodox Monks that are resident here are connected
with Mount Athos in Greece and very strict rules are followed.

AYIA EKATERINI CHAPEL ROYALE ★★

32kms northwest of Larnaka, 35kms south of Nicosia
At *Pyrga Village*; Open daily till sunset. If closed enquire for key in near by
coffee shop; Entrance Charge; Parking
A miniature of a building sitting next to a large modern church, this Medieval
chapel was build by King Janus in 1421, a wall painting of him and his wife
Charlotte de Bourbon is among a number of interesting wall paintings.

*Left: The Chapel Royal, situated in
front of the modern church;
Above; Medieval coat of arms
displayed inside the chapel*

89

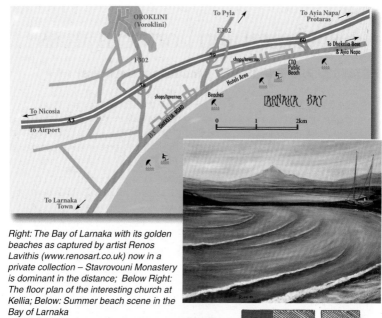

Right: The Bay of Larnaka with its golden
beaches as captured by artist Renos
Lavithis (www.renosart.co.uk) now in a
private collection – Stavrovouni Monastery
is dominant in the distance; Below Right:
The floor plan of the interesting church at
Kellia; Below: Summer beach scene in the
Bay of Larnaka

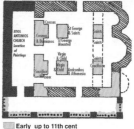

- [ ] Early up to 11th cent
- ■ 15th century   [ ] Of later periods
- [ ] 18th cent and recent extensions

AYIOS ANTONIOS CHURCH ★★

7kms to the north of Larnaka at Kellia Village Open during daylight. If locked,
ask for the village priest. Entrance Free (donation)
An important church built originally in the 9th century, extended and rebuilt
in later years.
The church was covered with numerous wall paintings which have been
recently cleaned and restored.

THE BAY OF LARNAKA / BEACHES ★★

Along the northern part of Larnaka coast towards the east and Ayia Napa.
The coast is dotted with apartments, hotels and the small new town which
serves tourist needs with shops, tavernas and bars.
Here are the sandy beaches with shallow waters that provide numerous water
sports. At the far top end the Tourist Office provides the **Public Beach of
Dhekelia** with facilities, cafeteria and parking. It is about 10kms from Larnaka
Town Tel: 24 64 45 11

90

useful telephones

InterCity Bus Co........... 24 64 34 92
to Paralimni/Protaras... 23 82 13 18
Bus to Ayia Napa.......... 23 72 13 21
Urban Buses.................... 24 65 04 77
Inter-City Taxis............... 24 66 10 10
First Aid.............................. 24 30 43 22
New Hospital.................. 24 80 05 00
Old Hospital..................... 24 30 43 12
Private Doctors 90 90 14 24
Chemists 24hrs................90 91 14 04
First Aid.............................. 24 30 43 22

Ambulance/Police/Fire.112 / 199
Athienou Health....   24 52 23 28
Kofinou Hospital............. 24 32 23 52
Lefkara Hospital............. 24 34 24 29

Ormidhia Health 24 72 15 72
Tersefanou Health 24 42 32 33

Police Headquarters.... 24 80 40 40
Fire Station........................ 24 80 42 80
Post Office...................... 24 80 24 50
Inland Transport 24 65 32 20
Harbour............................. 24 81 52 25
Water Authority............. 24 82 24 00
Airport Fire Service..... 24 80 43 50
Airport............................... 77 77 88 33
British Bases Police....... 1443
Religious Services
Anglican Church 24 65 13 27
Armenian Church......... 24 65 44 35
Catholic Mass 24 64 28 58
Greek Evangelical.......... 24 62 59 27
Jewish Synagogue.......... 24 82 87 70

distances

Distance from Larnaka town to:

	kms	miles
Nicosia.................	45	28
Limassol............................	71	44
Paphos........................	139	87
Polis.....................................	165	102
Troodos (via Limassol)	111	69
Ayia Napa.........................	41	25
Paralimni..........................	45	28

Distances from Larnaka Airport to:

Larnaka Town..................	5	2.5
Limassol............................	70	43
Paphos.........................	140	87
Ayia Napa.....................	50	31
Nicosia.............................	50	31

activities

Daktari Camel Park - Mazotos Village   Tel: 24 99 12 43
email: info@camel-park.com   web: www.camel-park.com   Open daily
all year round: cafe; restaurant; parking; facilities;   Entrance Charge
Horse Riding-Ponyland - Oroklini Village   Tel: 99 62 07 35
email: lovebirds@cytanet.com.cy
Drapia Farm, Kalavasos Village. Situated 2kms from Kalavasos, this facility
provides the exciting outdoor activity of horse riding in the countryside.
Tel: 24 33 29 98

*One of the most
popular landmarks
of Larnaka, Palm
Tree
Promenade with
its shops, cafes,
bars, restaurants
and the beach*

Ayia Napa-Protaras
golden beaches

The Sea Caves on the Eastern side of Ayia Napa

The two resorts are on the south and eastern sides of Cape Greco peninsula. Due to their unique beaches with golden sands and shallow waters, they have expanded into two major holiday destinations in Eastern Mediterranean.

AYIA NAPA is on the southern coast and offers endless beaches and a wealth of activities.

PROTARAS on the eastern side is an extension of the Famagusta coast which is further north and under occupation. It provides an equally varied and beautiful selection of beaches and water pursuits.

Inland, the "Red Villages" (Kokkinochoria), so called due to their fertile red soil which grows the famous Cyprus Potatoes, are dotted with picturesque villages and many churches and chapels.

Walking Tours

Depending on your location, these are easily worked out to meet your personal needs. Such short walks all along the coastline and through the centres of the tourist areas, mainly of Ayia Napa and Paralimni, can be pleasant and enjoyable.

Ayia Napa and the Sea - travel by bus, start at CTO information office; Tel : 23 72 17 96

Cavo Greco (Cape Greco) peninsula that has retained its natural state and it makes a rewarding walking tour along the rocky coastline (please do take care on rocks and cliffs). Here the Cyprus Tourist Office also arranges various routes for walkers. Visit www.visitcyprus.org.cy for updated details.

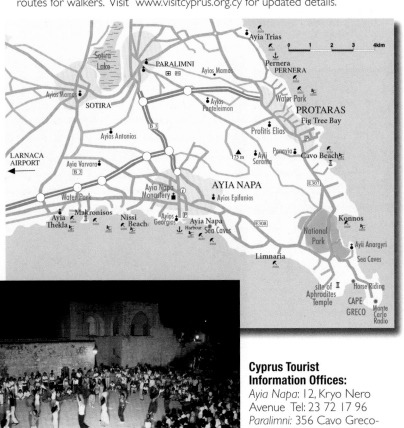

Cyprus Tourist Information Offices:

Ayia Napa: 12, Kryo Nero Avenue Tel: 23 72 17 96
Paralimni: 356 Cavo Greco-Protaras Ave
Tel: 23 83 28 65

Dancers at Ayia Napa Square, an annual, colourful festival

93

what to see and what to do
Ayia Napa resort

THE TOWN OF AYIA NAPA ★★★

About 41kms, 25miles to the east of Larnaka Town

The centre for night entertainment with discos, clubs, bars and eating places catering for every taste and pocket. Ayia Napa has established a name as a place of entertainment and enjoyment mainly for the young.

It also offers endless beaches with facilities and accommodation which caters for all pockets from top hotels to self catering apartments.

Daily sea trips around the coast during the summer is a must

Above: The Octagonal fountain in the courtyard of the Monastery; Right; A view of Ayia Napa Monastery; Below; Boats at Ayia Napa harbour

what to see around Ayia Napa

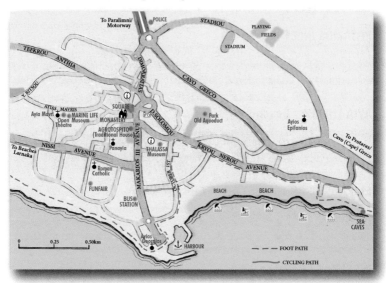

THE HARBOUR / Boat Trips ★★

A small fishing inlet has now grown into a central small harbour with boats, yachts and pleasure boats which offer short or long day trips along the coast and Cavo Greco peninsula. Around the harbour are numerous tavernas and cafeterias.

AYIA NAPA MONASTERY ★★★

In the centre of the village next to the main square. Open daily during day-time;   Entrance Free (donation for church)

Built by the Venetians around 1500, used occasionally by either monks or nuns and restored to its present state in the 1970's. It is the hub of an Ecclesiastical Centre for conferences and Religious Studies.

In the middle of tranquil gardens is an unusual Octagonal fountain with sculptural reliefs. The other attraction is the church which is cut into the rock that has been expanded with an outer facade. The bell tower is separate from the main structure.

MARINE MUSEUM ★★

An interesting collection in Marine life and paintings of marine scenes and It is worth visiting   **Thalassa - Museum of the Sea,** a combined display of the Pierides Foundation and George Tornaritis collections. It is regarded as one of the top European museums of its kind.

14 Kryo Nero Avenue   Tel: **23 81 63 66**   Entrance Charge
Open: Mon 09-13.00/ Tue-Sat: 09-17.00/ Sunday: 10-14.00
(July-Sept; Tue-Sun: 09-13.00 & 18.00-22.00)   Ideal for all the family

95

along the coast / beaches

POTAMOS INLET (Creek) ★★

14kms west of Ayia Napa, to the south of Liopetri village is an unusual inlet form the sea which extends into a river creek. It is the home of numerous colourful fishing boats moored along its banks with their multicoloured nets. Tavernas offer fresh fish and snacks; Parking.

AYIA THEKLA / Beach ★★

6kms west of Ayia Napa, a small whitewashed chapel. It is a shrine cut out of solid rock and the modern church stands by the shore. Here was once a Byzantine monastery. The beach is sandy protected from waves by a line of rocks in the water. Not as crowded as those near the resort.

MAKRONISSOS TOURIST AREA / Beach ★★★

In this area around 20 tombs dating to the Neolithic period were discovered near the Dome Hotel. An extended tourist area with hotels, apartments and eating places. A popular place due to its fine sandy beaches with three bays around a peninsula, offering facilities and shallow crystal waters.

NISSI BAY / Beaches ★★★

Just 3kms west of Ayia Napa, this was the earliest established tourist resort. A small rocky island connected with a sandy passage and perfect sandy beaches. It is one of the most popular resorts. All around are hotels, apartments and tavernas providing services and facilities.

AYIA NAPA BEACHES ★★★

Just to the east of the harbour, extending to the Grecian Bay Hotel area, these are golden beaches and very popular in the summer months.

SEA CAVES ★★

On the eastern outskirts of the town just below the cliffs. Clear waters add to the attraction of these unusual sea caves and rock formations.

LIMNARIA AREA / Beach ★★

4kms east of Ayia Napa, south of the main road is the Kermia Tourist Complex and by the sea there is a wonderful beach for all visitors which is protected by small rocks in the sea. Its a beautiful location to relax.

Ayia Napa beach scene

Three views of Ayia Napa coastal beaches. The golden sands and safe shallow waters attract visitors from all over the world

97

Protaras resort and coast

Coastal rocks in southern Protaras area

Boat trips are very popular

Extending from a long stretch of empty coves, bays and sandy beaches, south of the once major Tourist resort of Varosha (Famagusta) and visited occasionally by fishermen. Since the late 1970's the district has developed into one long Tourist resort with the central spot being The Fig Tree Bay area.

Hotels, Self Catering Apartments, Holiday Homes together with shops, tavernas, eating places for all tastes and bars have made this the alternative to Ayia Napa.

We start along the coast of Cavo Greco Peninsula and work up to the north...

CAPE GRECO PENINSULA ★★★

Spectacular rock formations, rocky coastline, clear water. Because of that it attracts many visitors who explore the peninsula on foot or with a bike... Inhabited by the ancients, the ruins of Temples were discovered. This a unique place to visit. If you are a good swimmer or a diver you can explore the waters around as well, but take care.

KONNOS BAY / BEACH ★★

To the north of Cavo Bay, just before Grecian Sands Hotel, a short twisting road takes you down to the bay and the sandy beach. Bus connection also from Protaras. Here are numerous watersports. Beds and umbrellas available on hire. A Tourist Office run cafe provides snacks and facilities.

PROTARAS - FIG TREE BAY BEACH ★★★

An exceptionally beautiful beach with spectacularly clear waters, with a small island in the middle of the Bay. Imagine this tourist centre being once just a fig tree, a taverna and a few fishing boats.

PERNERA BEACH / Fishing inlet ★★

On the northern part of the coast, this is again becoming a major Tourist area with its protected fishing harbour, from where short Boat cruises takes you up and down the coast.   The beach coves here are good for bathing.

AYIA TRIAS / Beach ★

The northern end of the coast before the occupied area of Famagusta. Just to the east of Paralimni. A small sandy bay, surrounded by numerous tavernas and a small chapel of Ayia Trias.

Above: The Bay and Beach of Konnos with its scenic coastline; Left: Fig Tree Bay's golden beaches

EXCURSIONS
out and about at Kokkinochoria and the coast

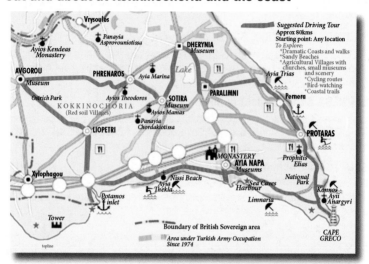

PARALIMNI ★★

This became the administrative centre of the area when all the services moved here after the occupation and desertion of Famagusta Town (Varosia). It has also grown into a tourist centre. It is only a short drive to the Protaras coast. The traditional old village square is an ideal place to visit with its numerous churches, some shops and tavernas.

DHERYNIA ★★

This village, 11kms from Ayia Napa, to the north of Paralimni is the closest place you can get to the proud old city of Varoshia. Here there are observation posts from where you get a glimpse of the ghost town of Varoshia and the occupied area.

At the **Cultural Centre** of Occupied Famagusta at 25 Evagorou Street there is photographic and other material on the subject. **Tel: 23 74 08 60** email: cultural.centre@cytanet.com.cy
Open: Mon-Fri 07.30-16.30/ Sat 09.30-16.30 Entrance Free

Also there is the **Dherynia Folkloric Museum** at 2 Demetri Liberty Street
Tel: 23 74 03 53 Open: Mon-Sat 09-17.00 Entrance Charge

SOTIRA VILLAGE ★★

One of the best known of "Kokkinochoria" (Red Soil Villages). In and around the village there are a number of churches and chapels to visit such as Ayios Mamas, Ayios Georgios Kortakion and Panayia Chordakiotissa. There is also a religious collection -**Ecclesiastical Museum** housed in a converted old chapel.
Tel: 23 82 39 32 for an appointment. Entrance Free.

AVGOROU VILLAGE ★★

To the northwest of Ayia Napa, around 19kms away and close to the occupied zone. There are a few interesting churches. The most important of which is Ayii Patros and Pavlos. Further north east is Ayios Kendeas now a nunnery and open to visitors by appointment Tel: 99 42 47 01

At Avgorou there is an interesting *Folkloric Museum* funded by the Pierides Foundation at 52 Karyon-Avgorou Avenue; **Tel: 23 92 33 40** Open; Mon-Fri: 08.30-13.00/ Wed & Thur also 16-18.00 in Jun-Oct (Nov-May 15-17.00) Sat: 09-13.00;   Entrance Charge.

PHRENAROS VILLAGE ★

Well known as an agricultural centre dating from Medieval times but also for the number of the churches in and around the village including: Ayia Marina; Archangelos Michael; Ayios Andronikos.

GRECO NATIONAL PARK ★★★

On the western side as you approach Protaras from the south, entrance opposite Konnos Bay.   It is an area of around 385 hectares and popular with visitors for its nature trails, peaceful surroundings and relaxation.

PROPHITIS ELIAS CHAPEL ★★

Despite its small, simplistic, modern Byzantine style architecture and due to its commanding position and the views of the resort and the sea, this small chapel is a major land mark in the area west of Protaras.

The fishing inlet of Potamos Liopetriou with its colourful atmosphere

useful telephones

Emergency Services........199
Famagusta Hospital.........23 20 00 00
Paralimni Hospital............23 82 12 11
Late 24hr chemists.........90 90 14 03
Private Doctors............90 90 14 23
Police / Ambulance ....112 / 199
Forest Fires.......................1407
Fire Service..........................23 80 32 32
......................................23 80 42 80
Water Service.............. ......23 82 13 23

Electricity........................ ......23 82 12 77
Ayia Napa Police 23 80 30 30
Dhekelia Bases..................443
Ayia Napa Post Office..23 72 15 50
Paralimni Post Office.....23 83 34 80
Pearl Bus Co..................23 82 13 18
EMAN Bus Co.............23 72 13 21
Urban Buses; 23 72 13 21
Paralimni.............................23 72 13 36
Taxis - Paralimni......... ......23 82 60 61
Religious Services
Anglican Church.......... ....23 81 10 45
Catholic Mass................24 64 28 58

distances

distances from Ayia Napa to

	kms	miles
Paralimni........................	9	5.5
Nicosia............................	80	50
Larnaka...........................	41	25
Limassol..........................	106	66
Troodos via Limassol	152	94
Paphos.............................	175	109
Polis via Paphos..............	197	123
Larnaka Airport..............	55	35
Paphos Airport...............	169	106

Above Top: Sunbather at Fig Tree beach; Above: Pernera fishing inlet. Fishing and short boat trips available from here

activities

Waterworld Waterpark - 18 Ayia Thekla Road, west Ayia Napa -For all the family- Facilities and Catering Tel: 23 72 44 44
email: contact@waterworldwaterpark.com   Entrance: Payable
www.waterworldwaterpark.com   Open: daily Mar-mid Nov: 10-18.00

Fun Waterpark - Protaras - Facilities; Catering - Tel: 23 83 38 88
email: andreas86@mailbox.gr Open: daily: Apr-Oct   Entrance Charge.

Flying Ostrich Park -10 Arch.Makarios Avenue, Avgorou - Tel: 23 92 28 59
Open: daily Summer: 08-22.00 ; Winter: 09-18.00   Entrance Charge

Ocean Aquarium -at Protaras Tel: 23 741111 email: ocean@cytanet.com.cy
Open: daily, all year round: 10.00-dusk   Entrance Charge

Magic Dancing Waters - Protaras Avenue children welcome Tel: 99 62 31 43 Open: Night show, at 21.00 May - Oct   Entrance Charge

Kikiriko Fun Park - 53 Nissi Avenue, Ayia Napa - a paradise for children
Tel: 99 69 39 55   Open: May - Sep 17-23.00

Parko Pallatso Fun Fair - off Nissi Avenue-for all the family Tel: 23 72 47 44
Open: evenings till late. Entrance Charge

Yellow Submarine - Ayia Napa Harbour Departs daily around 10.30; 12.15; 14.30 - A trip on a submarine along the coast.   Tel: 99 65 82 80

Riding - Moonshine Ranch by Cape Greco Tel: 99 60 50 42 Open: daily: 08-20.00 (or daylight)
Karting - EMG Go-Karts; Ayia Thekla, next to Waterworld Tel: 23 72 31 11
Open: 10-21.00

Dramatic coastline at Gape Greco area

Troodos
the mountain resorts

The freshness and beauty of the Troodos Forest attracts many visitors. Here, a view near Mesapotamos area

Troodos mountain region is the central bone of the island, a large area, it is dominant, impressive and endlessly beautiful, unique in the Mediterranean and in places, resembling a "Mini Swiss" mountain resort. Some of the highest peaks reach 3-4000ft above sea level and snow is not unusual in the winter months. It is a real paradise for nature lovers, walkers, botanists, painters, poets, lovers of Byzantine churches - all to be found in areas of breathtaking beauty.

In order to make it easier for you to follow such a large region, we follow the established regions, starting from **TROODOS -** central and south; **MARATHASA** - western side; **SOLEA** - to the north and **PITSILIA** - to the eastern part.

UNESCO - when we refer to churches with this word please note that these are now under the protection and funding of the World Cultural Heritage

Walking Tours / Nature Trails

Platres itself is an ideal place to walk around. However other resort centres also provide good walking. All can be planned and arranged individually.

The Cyprus Tourist Office has put together a wide ranging selection of nature trail suggestions, all included in a special publication.
ISBN 9963 44 037 1 obtainable only from the tourist offices or email: **cytour@cto.org.cy.** or visit the website: **www.visitcyprus.org.cy**

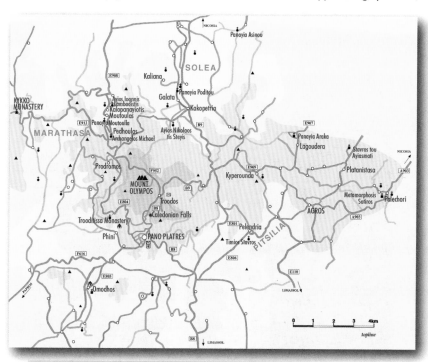

WHAT THE MOUNTAINS OFFER
<u>Bird Watching</u>: - Visit Troodos Visitor Centre, page 102
<u>Mountain Biking</u>:- Great way to explore around with freedom
<u>Hiking</u>: - To enjoy striking views / Join organised groups
<u>Skiing</u>: - Short Winter period at Mount Olympos
<u>Flora & Fauna:</u> - Well organised CTO Natural Trails, best way to explore
<u>Local Wineries:</u> - Southern mountain slopes, see pages 34 & 64
<u>Arts - Crafts - Traditions - Byzantine Richness</u>
for more.........
www.cyprusmountains.com

Cyprus Tourist Information Office:
Platres Square Tel: 25 42 13 16

what to see and what to do
TROODOS AREA

PANO PLATRES ★★★

39kms from Limassol. Situated just above Kato Platres, also known as Platres, is high up at 3,700 ft. It is the largest and most popular resort with a few hotels, apartments and eating places. A heavenly paradise buried in the greenery of the forest and orchards of Apple, Cherry and Pear trees. An ideal centre for walking, cycling and exploring.

PHINI (FOINI) ★★

4kms west of Platres, can be reached from the Kato Platres area, a very pretty village with a tradition of pottery and the sweet Delights. To see in the village:

Folk Art Museum and Pottery - Pylavakion,(privately run); Open most days during daylight; **Tel: 25 42 15 08** Entrance Charge.

Above: Snow covered mount Olympos (CTO);
Left: Caledonian Falls; Below: The charming and popular resort of Platres

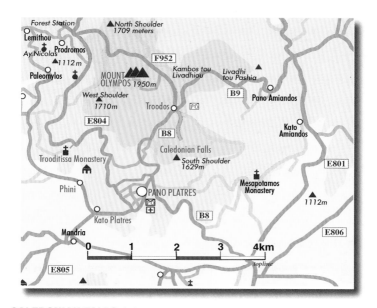

CALEDONIAN FALLS ★★

Half way between Platres (3kms) and Troodos, further east and reached only
on foot, this is one of the loveliest beauty spots with the biggest waterfalls in
the island. They are included in several of the trails.

TROODOS STATION / MOUNT OLYMPOS ★★★

It is called a station as this was once just a stopping place, with a couple of
buildings, before the climb to the summit. Now the square has expanded
with a few more buildings, mainly souvenir shops and cafe-restaurants. It is
also the starting point of nature trails and horse riding.

Troodos Visitors Centre is the ideal place for information, just 200 metres
west **Tel: 25 42 01 44** Open: Mon-Fri 10-15.00/ Sun 10-15.00/ Summer
to16.00.

Mount Olympos (also known as Chionistra in Greek), is the highest spot in the
island 1,952 metres (6,400ft) and a short drive from Troodos Square. It is believed that a temple dedicated to Aphrodite existed here. Now there are the
modern electronic listening installations of the British air defence system and
a powerful local TV tower. From such high spot the views of surrounding
areas and as far as the eye can see are breathtaking and it is worth the
visit. This area is usually covered by snow during some of the winter months.

TROODITISSA MONASTERY ★★

5kms from Platres, 40 kms from Limassol. Halfway along the southern road
between Platres and Prodromos, buried deep into the mountains in a beautiful setting amongst pine, walnut, cherry and apple trees, this old monastery
is dedicated to the Virgin Mary. Now the monastery is a retreat for resident
monks and closed to visitors except by appointment. The large square will
allow you to get a view of the area and the monastery and occasionally the
church is open to visitors.

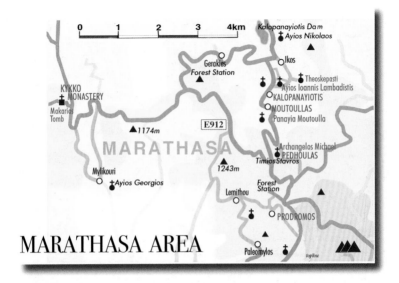

MARATHASA AREA

PRODROMOS / THEOTOKOS MONASTERY ★★

A popular resort during summer with idyllic settings and panoramic views, at 4,600ft it is probably the highest village in Cyprus.

The 13th century **Theotokos Monastery** (The Virgin of Trikoukia) was once a very big complex. It was abandoned and only recently restored into a convent with glorious views. It is 2kms to the south of Prodromos.
Tel: 25 46 27 47

PEDHOULAS / ARCHANGELOS MICHAEL ★★★ <u>UNESCO</u>

Set on the slopes in a beautiful valley and opposite the main road, this is another picturesque village with a commanding modern domed church in the centre of the village.

Archangelos Michael is a chapel dated to 1474 some 2kms above the village with a tiled roof. The interior is covered with beautiful wall paintings. To get in, ask at the village museum:

Archangelos Church Ecclesiastical Museum; Tel: **22 95 21 40**
Open daily Mar-Nov 10-18.00/ Dec-Feb 10-16.00   Entrance Charge

The **Folk Art Museum** in the village covers the history, culture and traditions of the whole of the Marathasa Valley; **Tel: 22 95 21 40**
Open Tue-Sun 10-16.00   Entrance Free

MOUTOULLAS / PANAYIA MOUTOULLA ★★ <u>UNESCO</u>

This attractive village built on the side of the mountain is to the north of Pedhoulas along the main road and is known for its clean refreshing spa water. The modern church is dominant in the village.

Panayia tou Moutoulla is the old church close to the village and dates to 1280 and contains many important icons and wall paintings. To visit, ask the local priest, or call at the coffee shop, **Tel: 22 95 23 41** or **22 95 26 77**

Above: A view of Ped-
houlas village;
Left: Wall painting of
Nativity at Archangelos
Michael church, Pedhoulas
Below: General view of
Moutoullas village

KALOPANAYIOTIS / AYIOS IOANNIS LAMBADISTIS ★★★ <u>UNESCO</u>

Some 69kms from Nicosia, western approach road. The last of the resort villages along the Marathasa valley is of medieval origin. It has a small spa and sulphur springs ideal for curing digestive disorders, problem skin and rheumatism. This is an artist's paradise with old houses and narrow winding streets.

Most important, it is one of the main Byzantine-Medieval churches in the island, a monastery of outstanding character and history - **Ayios Ioannis Lambadistis** - on the eastern side of the village and the river. It is a unique complex of three churches all under one roof: Ayios Herakleidios; St John Lambadistis (Ayios Ioannis); The Latin Chapel. A truly unique church and not to be missed. Attached to the church is an interesting

Byzantine Museum Tel: **22 95 34 60;**   Entrance Charge to museum; Open: Oct-Feb: Tue-Sat: 10-15.30; Sun: 11-15.30/ Mar-May & Sept: Tue-Sat: 09.30-17.00; Sun 11-17.00/ Jun-Aug: Tue-Sat: 09-13.00 & 15-19.00; Sun to 11

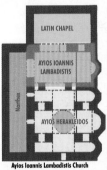

Ayios Ioannis Lambadistis Church

Ayios Ioannis Lambadistis church: Right: A wall painting of the Wise Men; Left: Floor plan of the church; Below: The church and the courtyard.

KYKKO MONASTERY / Byzantine Museum ★★★

12kms west of Pedhoulas; Opens daily during the daytime. Strict dress code; men, no shorts and must wear shirts or similar and ladies should cover their shoulders and not wear shorts either.

Parking in a large square, with facilities, shops of local produce and eating places. Avoid August 15 and the days around it as it gets very crowded.
Tel: 22 94 24 35

The biggest and richest monastic complex in Cyprus. It commands panoramic views of the surrounding valleys and as far away as the coastline to the west The views are even more spectacular from Throni about 3kms further up, where there is the tomb of Archbishop Makarios. The monastery is some 3,750ft above sea level and was believed to have been founded around 1092 by a hermit called Esaias. Its official religious name is *"The Holy Royal Stavropegaic Monastery of Kykko Founded With a Cross"*.

Having undergone various destructions and reconstructions over the years, the monastic buildings around the central courtyard are now covered by beautiful wall paintings. The church itself is a wonderful example of the richness of the Orthodox church with extremely beautiful icons and religious relics. Its free to visit when there is no service, (donation).

Kykko Byzantine Museum is within the monastery and very important for its collection of icons, Gospels, and religious objects beautifully displayed;
Tel 22 94 27 36;   Entrance Charge   Open Daily: Nov-May: 10-16.00/ Jun-Oct: 10-18.00

Two views of the most important of all, Kykko Monastery;
 Above: General view;
Left: The courtyard

111

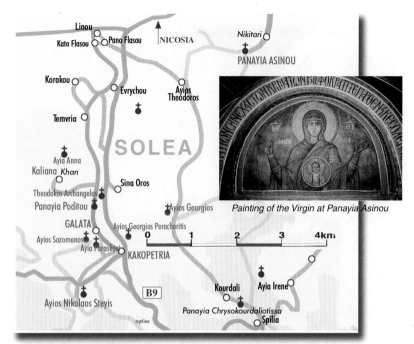

Painting of the Virgin at Panayia Asinou

SOLEA AREA

PANAYIA ASINOU ★★★ <u>UNESCO</u>

On the top eastern side, at the edge of the Solea area, just 5kms south of Nikitari village. Off the main Nicosia road to Troodos **Tel: 22 85 29 22 & 99 83 03 29** Entrance attendant Cafe open most of the year. Parking; Open daily:May-Aug: 09.30-17.00/ Sept-Oct: 09.30-16.30/ Nov-Apr: 09.30-16.00.

Dedicated to *Our Lady of the Pastures,* this church is one of the most famous in the island, with a past history. It is an old monastic settlement which does not exist any more. The wall paintings in such a small church are exquisite, some of the best examples of Byzantine art in Cyprus and they cover all the walls of the church. Not to be missed.

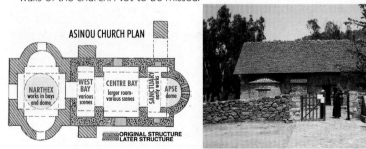

Left: Floor plan of Asinou church; Right: A view from the south

Left: Wall painting of Christ (Pantocrator) at Asinou church; Above: A fresco of the Holy communion at Panayia Podhitou at Galata; Below: A stream running through Galata village centre

GALATA / PANAYIA PODITHOU ★★★ <u>UNESCO</u>

In the northern part of the Solea Valley, buried in greenery and surrounded by mountains this was a major stopover place for those travelling from Nicosia to Troodos.

Also known as "Kaliana" which is nearby where there is a restored old Inn **"Hani Kaliana"**. The place is picturesque and has many churches, some medieval, some more modern. They include: Ayios Sozomenos in the centre of the village; Ayii Ioakim and Anna near Kaliana village; Panayia Theodokos also known as Archangelos Michael below the village. Near that is:

Panayia Podithou. This is the most important of the churches, dating to 1502 when it was a monastic complex. What remains is a small timber tiled roof and it contains excellent Italo-Byzantine style wall paintings, some regarded as masterpieces. It is situated just to the north of the village. To be able to visit you must ask for the local priest in the village square, or the local coffee shop; Tel: **22 92 23 94** or mob **99 98 50 49**

113

KAKOPETRIA / AYIOS NIKOLAOS TIS STEYIS ★★★ <u>UNESCO</u>

It is a lovely village, just south of Galata, a major summer resort with some hotels, shops, eating places. It is a place with peaceful surroundings and idyllic settings. Being a centre of silk making in medieval times, part of its old quarter is declared protected and has been restored.

Ayios Nikolaos tis Steyis is an extraordinary church, situated some 5kms to the west of Kakopetria and buried in the forest by the river Klarios. An 11th century church with later additions, contains excellent samples of paintings and icons. Situated in a beautiful pine gorge with scenic surroundings.

Open all year Tue-Sat 09-16.00/ Sun 11-16.00; Entrance Free (donation); Parking

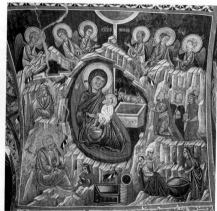

Ayios Nikolaos tis Steyis: Left: A view of the church; Right: 14th cent Nativity wall painting from the church;
Below: A bridge over the stream at Kakopetria resort

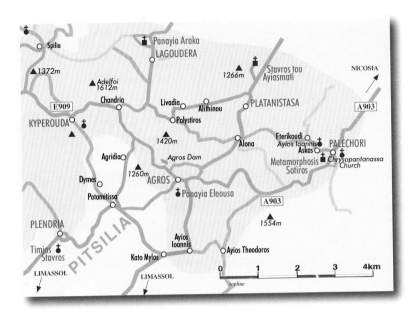

PITSILIA AREA

KYPEROUNDA / Museums ★★★

Some 40 minutes drive from Limassol, this is one of the largest villages in the mountains, tranquil, relaxing and with commanding views. The church of Timios Stavros is interesting. This medieval church also has the **Timios Stavros Church Museum**; to visit call Tel: **25 53 22 53** or ask for the priest Tel: **25 53 22 53** Also: Local community Board: Tel: **25 81 32 04**

Museum of Traditional Agricultural Life and Natural History, a collection of interesting items from the area: Tel: **25 81 32** 04

PLATANISTASA / STAVROS TOU AYIASMATI ★★ <u>UNESCO</u>

The village of Platanistasa is further east, some 30kms south of Nicosia and 15kms north of Agros. Surrounded by hills at a height of 1,000 metres above sea level, it offers superb views and outstanding scenery. There are numerous churches in the area, best known is:

Stavros tou Ayiasmati; about 15 minutes drive on a good surfaced road to the north of the village, off the main road to Nicosia. Open most days when an attendant is on the site. You can make a special appointment by calling the priest at Platanistasa coffee shop or the curator: Tel: **22 65 25 62** or mobile: Tel: **99 58 72 92;** Entrance Free (donation/contribution).

A fine example of 15th century single aisled church with steep timber roof. It contains excellent wall paintings and murals, being of post Byzantine style but also has a local Cypriot character. Icons are excellent as are the wood carvings and other religious objects. Additionally, the surrounding area is peaceful and relaxing and in the spring a paradise of wild flowers. It is worth the visit.

Stavros Ayiasmati (previous page):
Left: Nativity scene, wall painting
c.1494;
Below: A view of the church

LAGOUDERA / PANAYIA TOU ARAKA ★★★ <u>UNESCO</u>

This is a small village in the heart of Pitsilia some 15kms north of Agros, with exceptional views of ravines and mountain peaks.

Panayia tou Araka, near the village **Tel: 22 65 29 67** The priest resides in the building next to the church, available if needed.   Open daily: 09-15.00 (when attended) Entrance Free (donation); Parking; Facilities.

This is an outstanding 12th century church with a timber tiled roof. It contains some of the finest frescoes to be found in the island, many dating to 1192. All have been cleaned, restored and funded by the World Cultural Heritage. There are numerous other icons and wood carvings to be seen.

PALECHORI / Byzantine Museum /
METAMORPHOSIS TOU SOTIROS CHURCH ★★★ <u>UNESCO</u>

The jewel of the region, this is a large village where the centre is down in the valley with its traditional square. Seen from the top it resembles a southern Italian village with its red tiled roofs. It combines scenic beauty, unique architecture and traditional houses and is surrounded by vineyards and orchards of fruit trees. It is 45kms from Nicosia and 15kms north east of Agros. In a commanding position overlooking the village is an impressive statue representing a *Cypriot Mother.* A church to visit is *Panayia Chrysopantanassa,* it dominates the upper part of the village, by the square.

Church of Metamorphosis tou Sotiros (Transfiguration). A small rectangular church with a steep wooden roof on the hill just above the village. The walls are painted with post Byzantine-Cypriot style murals, some of the finest in the island. By the church is:

Museum of Byzantine Heritage; a fine collection of icons and religious relics. **Tel: 22 64 30 12;**   Entrance Free (donation) Open: Tue & Wed 10-13.00;

PANAYIA TOU ARAKA floor plan

NORTH WALL PAINTINGS

NARTHEX NAVE APSE

Panayia tou Araka: Above: Floor plan;
Right: Christ Pantocrator at the dome,
wall painting c.1192; Below: The church

Above Left: Panayia tou Araka wall painting of Nativity, c.1192; Above Right: 16th cent.wall
painting of Ayios Mamas from Metamorphosi Soteros church at Palechori; Below: An old
view of Palechori village

PELENDRIA / TIMIOS STAVROS CHURCH ★★ <u>UNESCO</u>

The large and beautiful village of Pelendria is in the southern section of Pitsilia, some 32kms from Limassol with some houses going back to medieval times. In the centre of the village is the 16th century **Panayia Katholiki Church** with interesting wall paintings. To visit call Tel: **25 55 22 68** mob **99 34 07 52**

Timios Stavros Church is near the village. An important medieval church which includes a Latin chapel. It contains many interesting 14th to 16th century wall paintings and it is worth a visit. Call for an appointment on Tel: **25 55 23 69**

In the village there is also a **Wine Museum** and a traditional working winery; Tel: **25 55 25 03** mob: **99 56 78 98** - appointment is preferable.

AGROS / PANAYIA ELEOUSA CHURCH ★★

A very important village of beauty and character. It is an essential place to visit and explore, and stay for a few days in the main hotel overlooking the village and the valleys. It is famed for its rose water and sweets, also smoked meats. It is about 45kms to the north of Limassol. Built on the side of the hill, its houses are traditional and the climb a bit steep.

In a dominant position in the lower part is **Panayia Eleousa**, a modern church built on the foundations of a much older one, it contains very interesting icons.

A panoramic view of the beautiful village of Agros

118

useful contacts

Kyperounda Hospital......25 53 20 21
Agros Hospital....................25 52 13 17
Evrychou Health 22 93 24 59
Kambos Health Care.....22 94 26 86
Platres Health 25 42 22 24
Palechori Hospital.............22 64 27 26
Pedhoulas Health 22 95 24 59
Cyprus Ski Club. 22 67 53 40
web: www.cyprusski.com

Cyprus Tennis Fed. 22 66 68 22
web: www.cyprustennis.com
Police / First Aid / Fire....112 199
Forest Fires...........................1407
Pedhoulas-Platres Bus.....22 95 24 37
Troodos-Kakopetria Bus...
....22 75 32 34
Kambos Bus via Kykkos...22 75 54 14
Troodos Camping.............25 42 02 05

distances

*Distances from Troodos Square, (which is
9kms -6miles from Platres).*

	km	miles
NICOSIA.........................	71	44
LIMASSOL.....................	45	28
PAPHOS.......................	113	71
POLIS, via Limassol....	148	92
LARNAKA	111	69
AYIA NAPA..................	152	95
PARALIMNI..................	156	97
LARNAKA Airport......	109	68
PAPHOS Airport..........	100	63

*Pelendria- Church of Panayia
Katholiki wall icon painting of the
Myrofores c.1500*

activities

The Troodos mountain resorts provide a great number of outdoor activities for both
children, families and the more adventurous travellers with a range of: Mountain Bikes;
Picnic sites; Natural Trails; Walking Tours; Mountain   climbing

*Walkers at
Troodos
mountain
slopes – the
best way to
explore and
admire its
beauty (CTO)*

119

Nicosia (Lefkosia)
the capital city

Eleftheria Platia (Liberty Square) – a popular landmark of Nicosia connecting the old walled city with the modern town - Plans are under way to modernise and upgrade the area

The biggest and most active city of the island, being the capital for over 1000 years, it is the centre of Political and Diplomatic life. All Government departments and ministries are based here. It is the cultural and commercial centre of the Republic.

It is a City of contrasts. All quarters inside the Walls have narrow streets and restored old houses. Then the sprawling city stretches in all directions with boulevards, shopping centres with modern shops and above all its excellent eating places providing quality local and international cuisine.

Sadly, Nicosia is also the only European City that is divided with the Turkish Cypriot Population living in the northern areas of the old city and beyond. They have been supported as a separate entity by the Turkish army of occupation since the 1974 invasion. Recently, entry points have been established allowing the free movement of people between the two sides. This is also encouraging cooperation in trade and cultural activities to take place which gives some hope for the re-unification of the City. We list in our book the major monuments which exist in the occupied sector with their old traditional names.

This is Nicosia, a capital city which attracts many visitors. Some to visit the Cyprus Museum and the Old Quarter of Laiki Yitonia, others to shop and others for cultural entertainment. It is also a centre for international business.

Walking Tours

We suggest, you select the place or places that interest you and work out your own itinerary around the locations as the length of time taken to see and explore depends on individual needs.

Alternatively, you can join one of the organised guided tours. - Within the City Walls around Chrysaliniotissa and Ayios Kassianos areas - Nicosia City Walls including Laiki Yitonia   - Town outside the Walls

Organised by the Tourist Office at Laiki Yitonia at No 11 Aristokyprou Street, Tel: 22 67 42 64 or other branches. They include: (i)- Chrysaliniotissa and Kaimakli guided bus and walking tour; (ii)- Old Nicosia guided walking tour; (iii) Outside the Walls, Modern Nicosia guided bus and walking tour

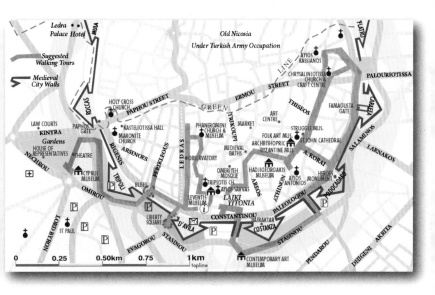

NICOSIA TOP ATTRACTIONS

Cyprus Tourist Information Offices:
Laiki Yitonia: 11 Aristokyprou Street Tel: 22 67 42 64
Head Office-Postal enquiries only: 19 Leoforos Lemesou, PO Box 24535
cy1390 Lefkosia email: cytour@cto.org.cy   web: www.visitcyprus.org.cy

what to see and what to do
museums; collections; galleries

CYPRUS ARCHAEOLOGICAL MUSEUM★★★

Mousiou Street, opposite Municipal Gardens **Tel: 22 86 58 64/ 86 58 88;**
Open: Tue-Fri: 08-16,00 (Thur to 17.00)/ Sat: 09-16,00/ Sun: 10-13.00
Entrance Charge

No visitor to the island with any interest in history or the past should miss this
unique collection of Cyprus' treasured past which stretches back into the mists
of time. The building with its neo-classical entrance has around 13 exhibiting
rooms starting from the Chalcolithic and Neolithic periods, through the
Bronze ages, the classical Greek, Hellenistic and Roman cultures up to the
early Christian period.

There is a wealth of exhibits, including pottery; vases; glassware; coins;
weapons; statuettes; statues, some life size. It contains many of the treasures
discovered at Salamis, the well known statue of Aphrodite, the bronze statue
of the Roman Emperor Septimius Severus, the Ayia Irene terracotta figurine
collection of around 2000 figures in different sizes.

A NEW MUSEUM FOR THE FUTURE
Plans have been approved to build a
New Ultra-modern Museum, bigger and
with more display space to meet the
21st century needs. The location is been
proposed to be on the site of the old
Nicosia hospital.

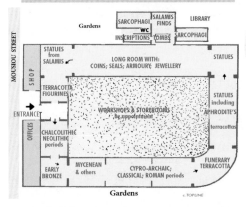

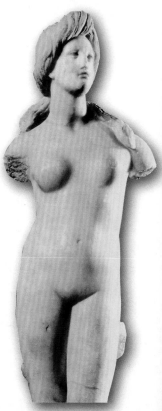

*Above: Floor plans of the Nicosia Museum best know
as CYPRUS MUSEUM;*
*Right: One of its most famous exhibits, that of the
statue of Aphrodite*

Above: The entrance to Cyprus Museum; Right: The 12th cent BC bronze statue of Horned God from Engomi;

Left: Ivory plaque from Salamis, 8th cent. BC;
Below: Many of the Terracotta figurines discovered at Ayia Irene (page 160),

LEVENTIS MUNICIPAL MUSEUM OF NICOSIA ★★

17 Ippocratous Street, Laiki Yitonia; **Tel: 22 66 14 75**
Open: Tue-Sun 10-16.30; Entrance Free (donation)

It presents the social and historical development of the capital going back to the early years up to the present day with a well displayed picture of medieval life and activities.

STATE COLLECTION OF CONTEMPORARY ART ★★★

Corner of Kritis Street and Leoforos Stasinou **Tel: 22 45 82 28**
Open: Mon-Fri 10-16.45/ Sat 10-12.45; Entrance Free

Housed in the the old Majestic Hotel building, it presents a unique collection of contemporary Cypriot artists from the 19th and 20th centuries to present day. This is the ideal place to to visit and assess the art movements of modern Cyprus.

NATIONAL STRUGGLE MUSEUM ★

7 Platia (Square) Arch Kyprianou **Tel: 22 30 58 78**
Open: Mon-Fri 08-14.00/ Thur also:15-17.30 except Jul-Aug Entrance Free

It exhibits historical documents, uniforms, paintings and photographs plus various objects and arms related to the Greek Cypriot struggle to liberate the island from its colonial rule in the 1950's.

ETHNOGRAPHICAL MUSEUM (FOLK ART MUSEUM) ★★★

Platia (Square) Arch. Kyprianos, within the old Archbishopric grounds, next to St John Cathedral; **Tel 22 43 25 78** Open: Tue-Fri 09.30-16.00/ Sat: 09-13.00 Entrance Charge.

It houses a very interesting collection of wood carvings; domestic tools; pottery; folk art, incl. embroidery and tapestry; local costumes. All exhibits of bygone times are displayed in numerous halls and rooms in this traditional old arched house.

BYZANTINE MUSEUM / ART COLLECTION ★★★

Part of the Archbishop Makarios III Cultural Centre and Foundation within the Archbishopric; Platia Arch. Kyprianos, behind St John Cathedral;
Tel: 22 43 00 08 Open Mon-Fri 09-16.30/ Sat 09-13.00; Entrance Charge
Photography is strictly prohibited.

It was the ambition of Archbishop Makarios, first President of the Republic, to establish a unique collection of Byzantine Art. He achieved this and it was completed after his death. Here you have the opportunity to admire some of the best examples of the Byzantine tradition of Cypriot icon painting dating as far back as the 8th century and extending to the 18th, some are of great artistic value and renown. Other influences coming from medieval times, such as the Frankish and Venetian schools, can be clearly seen in some of the icons.

Within the area of the Byzantine Museum there is a small but fine collection of Cypriot, Greek and European Fine Art from the 17th to the 19th centuries which also includes old prints, engravings, and maps.

Above: One of the rooms of the State Collection of Arts, with some of the fathers of contemporary painters;
Left: An icon from Phaneromeni Church-c14th cent, at the Byzantine Museum;
Left Bottom: Interior room of Ethnographical Museum;
Below: Leventis Municipal Museum, a portrait of Katerina Cornaro

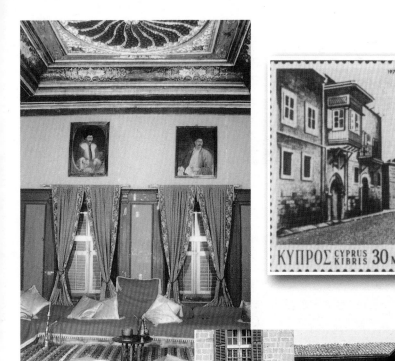

The House of Hadjigeorgakis Kornesios: A stamp showing the exterior; An interior room; The courtyard of the House

HOUSE OF HADJIGEORGAKIS KORNESIOS - The Dragoman ★★★

(Ethnological Museum) 20 Patriarch Gregorios Street   **Tel: 22 30 53 16**
Open: Mon-Fri 08.30-15.30/ (early closing, Mon to14.00 and late closing on Thur to 17.00)   Entrance Charge

A well preserved 18th century building, the house of Dragoman (Interpreter to the Turkish court - an important position) Hadjigeorgakis Kornesios has now been restored with funds from Europa Nostra. It makes an interesting period museum .

The cool courtyard with its stone fountain leads to the gardens and the various rooms which display period furniture, carved wood work and the reconstructed "Reception Room" - a divan-lined room for formal receptions. A visit to this place can be rewarding and its only 5 minutes walk from the Archbishopric.

NICOSIA MUNICIPAL ARTS CENTRE ★

19 Apostolos Varnavas Street **Tel: 22 43 25 31 / 79 74 00**
Open: Tue-Sat: 10-15.00 & 17-23.00/ Sun 10-16.00 and during exhibitions
advertised.   Entrance Free.   Associated with the Pierides Museum of
Contemporary Art in Athens, it is housed in the old power station and it
organises regular exhibitions and art events.

POSTAL AND PHILATELIC MUSEUM ★

3B Ayios Savvas Street, **Tel: 22 30 47 11**
Open: Mon-Fri 09-15.00/ Sat 09-13.00;   Entrance Free
Philatelic and Postal history of Cyprus Postal services including displays of
stamps.

COINAGE MUSEUM HISTORY ★

51 Stasinou and Ayias Paraskevis Str. **Tel: 22 67 71 34**
Open: Mon-Fri 08-14.00 (Sep-Apr on Mon 08.30-17.00) Entrance Free -
Bank of Cyprus Headquarters Centre
A permanent exhibition of the history of Cyprus coinage dating from the
6th century BC to present day.

CYPRUS GEOGRAPHICAL MUSEUM

79A Archbishop Kyprianos Avenue, Strovolos **Tel: 22 47 03 40**
Open: Mon-Fri 07.30-14.30 (Thur to 18.00) Entrance Charge
An 18th cent Inn converted and exhibits the history of Cyprus Geology,
Flora and Fauna, worth a visit.

CYPRUS MUSEUM OF NATURAL HISTORY ★

Carlsberg Brewery Grounds - Latchia, eastern Nicosia **Tel: 22 47 11 11**
;Open: Mon-Fri 09-16.00; Entrance Free
It displays over 2500 exhibits.

CLASSIC MOTORCYCLE MUSEUM ★★

44 Granikou Street, Old Nicosia; **22 68 02 22** email: x.n@cytanet.com.cy;
Entrance Charge   Open: Mon-Fri 09.30-13.00 & 15.30-19.00/ Sat 09.30-
13.00   Over 150 classical machines all well preserved. One of the largest
collections in the world awaits enthusiasts.

GEORGE AND NEFELI GIABRA (Pierides Collection)★★

Phaneromenis Street, next to the church **Tel: 22 67 71 34**
Open: Mon-Sat: 10-17.00; Entrance Free
A fine collection, mainly of pottery through the ages donated by Clio and
Solon Triantafillides.

CYPRUS POLICE MUSEUM ★

Within the Police Headquarters **Tel: 22 80 87 93**; Open Mon-Fri 08-14.00;
Entrance Free www.police.gov.cy

VON WORLD PENS HALL ★

37 Demostheni Severi Ave. **Tel: 22 46 32 04** Entrance charge
www.vonpenshall.com; em: von@vonpenshall.com

127

medieval places and monuments

THE CITY WALLS ★★★

These formidable Venetian fortifications surround the old city of Nicosia and many parts have been preserved and in several places are in excellent condition.

A walk around the walls from the Paphos Gate, on the west side to the Famagusta Gate to the east is a pleasant experience (avoid hot summer days), and many parts of the moat are now green spaces, good for relaxation.

The walls were constructed by Francesco Barbaro in 1567 and encircled the city. There were 11 bastions, all of which survived including the three important gates: to the north is Kyrenia Gate, to the southwest is Paphos Gate and to the east is Famagusta Gate.

The invading Ottoman Turks commenced their siege on 26 July 1570 and it was captured on September 9th. According to reports, over 20,000 of the inhabitants were killed and others sold as slaves. Much of the city was burned.

Kyrenia Gate - (Porta del Proveiore) is within occupied Nicosia. It was restored in 1821 and a domed room was added. It is a gateway to Kyrenia and the Castles high up in the mountain range in the north.

Paphos Gate - (Porta di San Demenico) is a short walk from the Nicosia Museum but it is right on the dividing Green Line and its Roccas Bastion is manned by the occupying army. Viewing of the structure is better from the roundabout on the road below.

Famagusta Gate - (Porta Guiliana) is the most important of the three gates, the strongest and the principal gate. An impressive structure, it includes several halls which are used as a Cultural Centre for exhibitions, conferences lectures and performances. Pyli Amochostou-Leoforos Athinon **Tel: 22 43 08 77** Open: Mon-Fri 10-13.00 & 16-19.00 (May-Sep 17-20.00) and when events and exhibitions take place; Entrance Free

KASTELIOTISSA MEDIEVAL HALL ★★

Opposite Paphos Gate, in the free areas. Originally part of the Lusignan Palace and built in gothic architectural style, it is now used for events and exhibitions as advertised.

Part of the City Walls near Famagusta Gate

128

Medieval Nicosia

BARBARO

GURINI

KYRENIA GATE

LOREDANO

HULA

site of 3rd Royal Palace

Ayios Loukas

Yeni Jami Mosque

FLATRO

Venetian Column

Haydarpasa Mosque

St Claire Convent

Carmelites Church

Iplik Bazari Mq

(St. Katherine)

Benedictine Convent now Armenian Ch.

Beuyuk Haman

Selimiye Mosque (St Sophia)

Bedestan (St Nicholas)

Chrysaliniotissa Greek Mon.

ROCCAS

Beuyuk Khan

CARAFFA

Franciscan Mon now Catholic Ch.

GREEN LINE

FAMAGUSTA GATE

PAPHOS GATE

site of 2nd Royal Palace

site of Lusignan Palace

TRIPOLI

Augustian Monastery (Omeriyeh Mosque)

PODOCATARO

LAIKI YITONIA

D'AVILA

COSTANZA

0   0.25   0.50km   0.75   1km

Above: Famagusta Gate, now a major cultural centre; Below: Two views from the Walls

churches and religious places

ST JOHN CATHEDRAL (Ayios Ioannis) ★★★

Platia (Square) Archbishop Kyprianos - grounds of Archbishopric; Entrance Free (donation)   Open Mon-Fri 08-12.00 & 14-16.00/ Sat 08-12.00

Once a Benedictine Abbey it became an Orthodox monastic centre in 1426. The existing church was built in 1662 under Archbishop Nikeforos. The interior is covered with exquisite wall paintings, magnificent frescoes, wood carvings and icons which are all worth seeing.

This the Orthodox Cathedral of Nicosia where the island's Archbishops are enthroned and other important religious services take place. At these times the church closes to visitors.

Holy Archbishopric, Archbishop Kyprianos Square **Tel 22 55 46 00**

Saint John Cathedral; Behind it is the Byzantine Museum and on the right the Ethnographical Museum;
Right; A painting of Nativity inside the church

PHANEROMENI CHURCH ★★

Onasagorou Street, end of Ledra Street, near Green Line, Open daily during daylight hours except when mass takes place. Entrance Free (donation)

A large and impressive church built in 1872 on the ruins of a medieval nunnery. Within the church are the remains of the victims of the Turkish purge of 1821 in a special mausoleum. Inside the church there is a fine collection of icons, relics, and grand chandeliers plus a beautifully carved 17th century iconostasi.

The church and the surrounding buildings, including the small *Arabian Mosque* next to the church, make lovely places to visit and wander around.

TRIPIOTIS CHURCH ★★

47 Solonos Street, near Laiki Yitonia; Open daytime at irregular times. Entrance Free (donation) A Franco-Byzantine style church built in 1695 with a rich interior of icons and religious relics.

Above: A view of Tripiotis church in Old Nicosia – a view from the Ledra Observatory;
Left: Part of Phaneromeni church

AYIOS KASSIANOS CHURCH ★

Within the City Walls on the eastern side close to the Green Line. Open irregularly; Entrance Free (donation) It was built in 1854 on the ruins of a previous Latin Church. Famed for its beautiful icons, many have now been moved to the Byzantine Museum for protection.

CHRYSALINIOTISSA CHURCH / CRAFT CENTRE ★★

Chrysaliniotissa Odysseos Str., north of Famagusta Gate. Open during daylight when attended; Entrance Free. One of the oldest Byzantine churches in Nicosia dating to 1450, dedicated to "Our Lady of the Golden Flax" and restored to its old glory with wall paintings, icons and wood carvings.

This neighbourhood has been revitalised with cafes, tavernas and the *Chrysaliniotissa Crafts Centre*, corner of Ipponaktos and Dimonaktos Streets. Tel: **22 34 80 50**, mob **99 62 96 11** Entrance Free   Open: Mon-Fri 09-13.00 & 15-18.00 (May-Sep 16-19.00)/ Sat: 10-13.00;   Functioning workshops of traditional crafts are situated around a courtyard which has been designed in the style of an old Inn

BAIRAKTAR MOSQUE ★

Constanza Bastion, southern side; Closed to visitors. Here lies the memorial Mosque on the spot where the first Ottoman soldier fell carrying the flag.

OMERIYEH MOSQUE ★★

Trikoupi and Tyllirias Square, opposite Omeriyeh Baths   Open for prayers; visitors allowed at reasonable time, when no prayers are taking place; Entrance Free (donation). Built in the 14th century as the church of St Mary, an important medieval Lusignan place of worship, it was converted into a mosque after 1571 and now used by the moslem community of Nicosia.

ST PAULS ANGLICAN CATHEDRAL ★
Leoforos Lord Byron Tel: 22 44 22 41/67 78 97 Open for prayers and visits

HOLY CROSS ROMAN CATHOLIC CHURCH
Near Paphos Gate Tel: 22 66 21 32

Ayios Savvas church near Laiki Yitonia

Above: Old Nicosia street near Chrysaliniotissa church;
Left: The restored church of Chrysaliniotissa;
Below: Omeriyeh Mosque

133

other places of interest

LAIKI YITONIA ★★★

The typical Cypriot neighbourhood with the traditional houses and narrow streets of bygone times. Here, in the walled part of the old city of Nicosia, a whole area has been renovated and has become of the most popular places in the whole island. In the narrow pedestrianised streets there to browse in and explore, there are souvenir and gift shops, bookshops with old editions and maps, Cafes, bars and the traditional Tavernas. It is a place not to be missed, very near Eleftheria Square.

MUNICIPAL GARDENS / Theatre House of Representatives ★★

The most significant green space of Nicosia, opposite the Cyprus Museum, relaxing and beautifully landscaped. On the eastern side is the Neo-classical building of the *Municipal Theatre* where major musical and theatrical events take place. On the western side of the gardens is the impressive building of *The House of Representatives* and visitors are allowed to view Murals in the Foyer.

ELEFTHRIAS PLATIA (Liberty Square) / LEDRA STREET ★★

The wide square which once linked Old Nicosia with the new, modern city next to D'Avilla Bastion. The square is famous for its various rallies and demos also for its colourful kiosks. Leading from the square is Ledra Street, once the commercial heart of the city. Also a meeting place for poets, writers and artists. It still retains some of its colourful shops, cafeterias (Kafenio) and is now pedestrianised.

LEDRA MUSEUM AND OBSERVATORY ★★

Half way down Ledra Street, Shakolas Tower Building - Look Out Tower, 11th Floor **Tel: 22 67 93 69**   Open: Apr-Oct Mon-Sun 10-20.00/ Nov-Mar Mon-Sun 09.30-16.00;   Entrance Charge

It provides a panoramic view over all Nicosia including the old city, part of which is occupied, with its medieval monuments. It also provides a photographic history of the city.

HEROES MONUMENT (Liberty Monument) ★

Podocataro Bastion, on the eastern side, a complex of sculptures dedicated to the fighters and the people who participated in the struggle for independence in the 1950's.

THE ARCHBISHOPRIC ★★

Platia Archbishop Kyprianos; Visits by appointment, **Tel: 22 55 46 00**

A modern refreshing building, it is the work of George Nimikos, a Greek architect. It was started in 1956 and completed in 1960 and became the official residence of the Archbishops of Cyprus, Makarios III being the first resident. Outside the iron gate next to St. John's Cathedral is the bust of Archbishop Kyprianos who was hanged in 1821 during the Turkish purge.

OMERIYE BATHS (Hamam) ★★★

Next to Omeriye Mosque, 8 Tyllirias Square, **Tel: 22 46 05 70** and 22 **75 05 50** Medieval baths recently restored. Conducted tours every 20 minutes on Mondays

Above: Monument to the Heroes of the struggle for Independence (Liberty Monument);
Below Left: Part of the restored Omeriye Baths;
Below Right: The modern Municipal Theatre

11-17.00pm, entrance charge. Working baths can be used and health treatments are available at extra charge. For men: on Tuesdays; Thursdays and Saturdays, 09-21.00 For women: on Wednesdays; Fridays and Sundays, 09-21.00

ATHALASSA FOREST PARK-VISITORS CENTRE ★★

East of the old road to Limassol on the south east outskirts of Nicosia;
Open Mon-Fri: 07.30-14.30 (Thur also 15-18.00) Entrance Charge to Visitors Centre: **Tel: 22 46 29 43**

Some 840 hectares of parkland and forest, with nurseries, botanical gardens, a landscaped lake, picnic areas and a number of organised Nature Trails arranged by the Cyprus Tourism Organisation.

LEDRA PALACE HOTEL ★

Leoforos Marcou Drakou - near Paphos Gate Once it was the most popular hotel in the Middle East, elegant and full of life. After the invasion of 1974 it went silent and was then established as a base for the UN peacekeeping force. A check point is also here between the two areas. Its worth a visit up to the hotel to get a glimpse of its glorious past.

135

shopping

Nicosia is a shoppers paradise. From souvenirs, reproduction antiques and books in the old quarter of Laiki Yitonia to the famous shopping artery of the old town **Ledra Street.** This was the famous street of the post World War II decades. A place of commerce and social activity which lasted till 1974. Now it has been pedestrianised, it is the perfect shopping place for a stroll and a coffee at numerous cafes.

Also in the main streets, mainly Archbishop Makarios III Avenue and the department stores in and around it, you will enjoy shopping for the latest designer clothes and quality leather goods.

CYPRUS HANDICRAFT CENTRE ★★

186 Leoforos Athalassas, southern part of Nicosia, Tel: 22 30 50 24
Open: *workshops* Mon-Fri 07.30-14.30 & 15-18.00
shops Mon-Sat 08-13.00 & 14.30-17.30 (Jul-Aug 17-19.30)
A Government run enterprise that encourages the continuity of producing quality traditional folk arts and crafts and preserving the old skills.

Enjoy a visit to the colourful *Outdoor Markets* of Nicosia
- Wednesday mornings at Constanza Bastion
- Central Market Old Municipality at Dimarchion Square in the old city
- Municipal market of Ayios Antonios, junction Dhigeni Akrita

Laiki Yitonia, just one corner......

136

EXCURSIONS
from south to west

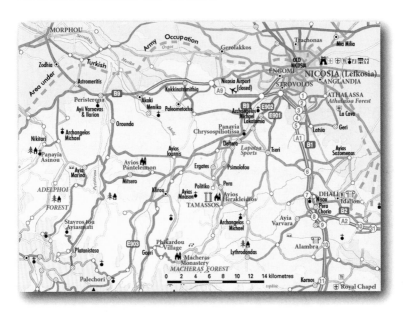

DHALI (IDALION) / ANCIENT SITE ★★

The expanding village of Dhali is off the motorway towards Larnaka. About 20kms southeast of Nicosia.

In and around the village are numerous churches as Ayii Apostoloi to the west, Ayios Georgios to the south and within the village is Ayios Demetrios.

The Ancient Kingdom of Idalion is situated near the village, but due to its close proximity to the occupied zone the site is currently closed to visitors.

The Kingdom of Idalion was once predominant in this area. It existed from the Bronze Age well into 400 BC. There is a strong tradition that the city was founded by Chalcanor, one of the heroes from the Trojan Wars. The city was

From ancient Idalion: Above, a silver coin during the period of King Kra;
Right: Female head statuette c.5th century BC,
(Cyprus Museum)

137

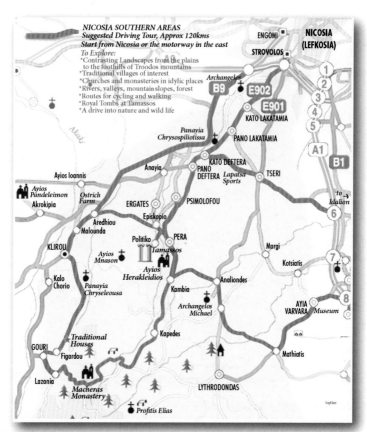

NICOSIA SOUTHERN AREAS
Suggested Driving Tour, Approx 120kms
Start from Nicosia or the motorway in the east
To Explore:
*Contrasting Landscapes from the plains
 to the foothills of Troodos mountains
*Traditional villages of interest
*Churches and monasteries in idylic places
*Rivers, valleys, mountain slopes, forest
*Routes for cycling and walking
*Royal Tombs at Tamassos
*A drive into nature and wild life

full of temples, some 14 in all but the most important were those of Aphrodite, Apollo and Athena. The Phoenicians became very influential and established a strong commercial presence. Some city walls, chambers and temples can still be seen. The Palace of Idalion has been unearthed in recent excavations and is located on the western side of Ambeleris Hill. It was built at the beginning of the Cypro-Archaic period and was also widely used by the Phoenicians. The Palace is believed to date to the 8th.-7th. century BC and was still in use during the Hellenistic period.

Local Museum of Idalion. Just recently opened, it houses an array of finds from this important Kingdom, situated close to the ancient site.

PANAYIA CHRYSOSPILIOTISSA (Virgin Mary's Golden Cave) ★★

Situated to the north of Deftera village, 11kms south of Nicosia;   Open daily during daytime;   Entrance Free

A cave on the side of a hill on the left bank of Pedhieos river, perhaps an early Christian hermitage and a place for pilgrims.

AYIA VARVARA VILLAGE, ★ south of Nicosia
Proto-Industrial Museum; Tel 22 52 17 15 by appointment

ANCIENT SITE OF TAMASSOS / Royal Tombs ★★★

17kms (10miles) south of Nicosia, near Politico village **Tel: 22 62 26 19**
Open Daily: Nov-Mar 08.30-16.00/ Apr-Oct: 09.30-17.00 Entrance Charge

One of the most important Kingdom Cities of ancient Cyprus. The area became important after the discovery of copper around 2500 BC and the rich mines brought power and prosperity to the whole area. 'Temese' (another name for Tamassos) was mentioned in Homer's Odyssey when Athena went in quest of copper. By 800 BC it became an important Phoenician colony and a kingdom. After his victory at Tyre (322 BC), Alexander the Great gave the mines to Phytagoras, King of Salamis. Then in 12 BC King Herod the Great of Palestine took a lease on the majority of the Cyprus copper mines. Administration was in the hands of the priests who formed an elite class as the mines were deemed to be a "Gift of the Gods".

The most important finds include those of the *Royal Tombs* although they had been badly looted in the past. Two of the Royal Tombs are in excellent condition. Other finds including factories where the copper was processed and some residential quarters, believed to be those of the ruling class, they give us some idea of their living conditions. Many of the items discovered are in the British Museum and the Cyprus Museum.

Left: One of the Royal Tombs of ancient Tamassos;
Above: A statue of a Sphinx dating to c.500 BC (Cyprus Museum);
Below: Various plans of Tombs

TAMASSOS ROYAL TOMBS

FIRST ROYAL TOMB

Entrance with monumental Propylaeum of flat roof. A flight of 22 steps leads to tomb supported by monoliths and Proto Ionic Capitals.

The second of two Burial Chambers. Both of these Chambers have carved roofs.

SECOND ROYAL TOMB

Entrance (Propylaeum) is supported on either side by a carved monolith with Proto-Ionic Capitals. The 12 original steps have been preserved.

The Burial Chamber roof is saddle-shaped. It consists of te large slaps resting on the side walls. Paved floor with slabs

AYIOS HERAKLEIDIOS CONVENT ★★

Just 5 minutes drive to the south of Tamassos   **Tel: 22 62 39 50**
Open for group visits - Mon. Tue and Thurs 09-12.00 midday. To visitors day
light (closed 12 noon-15.00)   Photography is not allowed.
Entrance Free (donation);   Dress code

It was built around a Roman Tomb and it originated in the early Christian
period then was rebuilt in later years. The present church dates from 1759.
The establishment of an early Christian church here is due to Ayios
Herakleidios who was the first bishop and was appointed by Saints Paul and
Barnabas. It was a centre of early Christianity.

The two aisled church is in the courtyard surrounded by the living quarters
of the convent. Run by nuns, it was renovated in 1773 and includes a beautiful, flower filled courtyard. The nuns produce splendid rose jams and glygo
amygdalo (sweet almond preserve).

*The Dome of
Ayios Herakleidios
Convent*

MACHERAS MONASTERY (Panayia Machera) ★★★

41kms south of Nicosia **Tel: 22 35 93 34/5**   Open Daily: 08.30-17.30/ For
groups Mon-Tue-Thur 09-12.00   Cafe opens occasionally in the square;
Dress code   Photography not allowed; Entrance Free (donation)

Situated by the slope of Mount Kionia near the source of the Pedieos river in
idyllic and beautiful surroundings in the forest. The name was given to the
foundation because a miraculous icon of the Virgin Mary was found nearby in
a well, pierced with a knife (Macheri) which gives it the name.   It was founded
in the 12th century. It was rebuilt in its present state in 1900 and is a wealthy
establishment which profits from the rich land that surrounds it. In more recent times the monastery became known for harbouring EOKA fighters during the Independence struggle of 1955-59. The much revered second in
command, Gregoris Afxentiou, was found hiding in a cave in the hills nearby
where he was eventually killed. A small museum is dedicated to the hero.

There are numerous well preserved icons and relics to be seen, also an old
Gospel printed in Venice in 1588, a book 'Explanations of the Gospel' dated
1792 plus an icon of the Virgin Mary which was discovered in a cave and is
protected by a sword. The church was built in the middle of a courtyard surrounded by the living quarters, a library and the museum. It is one of the oldest and most important foundations. During the Turkish Ottoman occupation
it was a centre of Christian Orthodox Education.

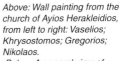

Above: Wall painting from the church of Ayios Herakleidios, from left to right: Vaselios; Khrysostomos; Gregorios; Nikolaos.
Below: A general view of Machera Monastery surrounded by pine forest
Right: Kionia peak, south of the monastery, one of the highest in Troodos, 1423m

PHIKARDOU VILLAGE / Rural Museum / Gouri ★★★

40kms south of Nicosia, near Klirou village   Tel: 22 63 47 31
Open Daily: Nov-Mar 08-16.00/ Apr-Oct: 09-17.00
Entrance Charge   Parking; Cafe: most of the time.

This whole village has been declared a protected area by the department of Antiquities. It is a picturesque place with houses in the old style some of which are preserved and listed as monuments of traditional architecture. One of the best known is the *"House of Katsinioros"*, part of which is dated to the 16th. century. In 1987 it received, together with other houses such as the *"House of Achilleas Dimitri,"* the *Europa Nostra* award for restoration. They are living museums of rural architecture.

About 1.5kms west of Phikardou, which is also architecturally protected, is the village of **Gouri** famous for its old traditional buildings. Some of its 18th century houses contain some fine woodwork.

Left: Phikardou Village, an early stage restoration of old houses, the project now has many properties restored;

Below: The interesting church of Peristerona which contains beautifully executed icons

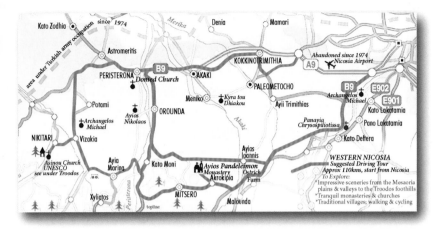

AYII BARNABAS AND HILARION CHURCH - PERISTERONA ★★

27kms west of Nicosia, on the main Nicosia-Troodos road Open: most of times - if not key is at the nearby cafe - Parking; Coffee shops nearby.

It dominates the eastern banks of the now dry river on the eastern side of Peristerona village. Its architecture is unusual as it has five domes and three aisles. Although similar to that of Ayia Paraskevi in the Geroskipos village in Paphos, this is the only one in Cyprus to have so many domes.

It dates to the 10th century with later restorations. The interior of the church has good icons, an iconostasi, wood carvings and other relics. The doors on the western side have the original Byzantine style frames.

AYIOS PANTELEIMON ACHERAS CONVENT ★

1.5kms northwest of Agokipia village, western side   **Tel: 22 63 23 45**   Occasionally Open: Free (donations) preferably visits by appointment.

It has a rectangular church which was restored in 1770. It is now a convent and contains some interesting wood carvings and icons.

The western site of the Mesaoria plain, fields with wheat

143

Above Left: A roundabout fountain in Nicosia by the walls; Above Right: Afternoon siesta, two shopkeepers relaxing with a game of backgammon;
Below; The Palace of the Archbishop of Cyprus next to Saint John's Cathedral (page 130)

activities

Ostrich Wonderland Farm

Tel: 22 99 10 08/9 email: ostrich@logos.cy.net   Open: daily: May - Oct: 09-19.00 ; Nov - Apr:09-17.00 Entrance: Payable Facilities; Car Park; Refreshments

This is the biggest farm of its kind in Europe and is situated some 25 mins. drive to the southwest of Nicosia at Ayios Ioannis Maloundas.

Lapatsa Sports Centre

Tel: 22 62 12 01/2/3   A county club and sports centre, one of the biggest in the Middle East, situated only 15 mins. drive from Nicosia. It provides a riding school, five tennis courts and one of the best equipped swimming pools in Cyprus. Restaurants.

Nicosia Race Club

at Ayios Dhometios suburb, south of Nicosia Tel: 22 78 27   email: infor@nicosiaraceclub.com.cy   web: www.nicosiaraceclub.com.cy

There are regular races every Sunday except in June and July when they take place on Saturdays. There are 'All Star' races in early March when international jockeys are invited to participate.

useful telephones

Nicosia Gen. Hospital ...22 60 30 30
Makario Hospital............22 40 50 00
Thalassoemia Centre.... 22 40 50 50
Chemists 24hr.................. 90 90 14 02
Private Doctors...............14 22
First Aid.............................22 80 14 75
Akaki Health Care..........22 82 10 80
Dhali Hospital..................22 52 19 22
Klirou Health Care........ .22 63 23 32

Police Headquarters......22 80 20 20
Police General..................14 60
Post Office.......................22 80 57 19
Electricity Authority.......22 84 50 00
Water Authority.............22 69 80 00
Fire Service.......................22 80 21 50
British Council.................22 58 50 00
French Cultural Cent.....22 45 93 33
Russian Cultural Cent...22 76 16 07
American Centre...........22 67 71 43
Goethe Institute.............22 66 66 14

Transport...........................22 66 58 14
Inter-urban Bus Co........22 66 58 14
Inter-city Bus-Larnaka .22 66 58 14
Nea Amoroza-Paphos 26 93 68 22

Urban Buses.................. ....22 66 58 14
Troodos Mountains........99 61 88 65
Kykko Monastery To,......99 62 36 04
Inter-city taxi 22 73 08 88
Religious Services
Anglican Church 22 67 78 97
Catholic Mass 22 66 21 32
Armenian Church 22 49 35 60
Greek Evangelical 22 66 47 29
German Evangelical at St Pauls Anglican
Maronite Church 22 67 88 77
Muslim Faith at Omeryie Mosque
Libraries
Ministry of Education - Konstantinou
Palaelogou Str. 22 30 31 80

Nicosia Municipal Art Centre Library -
19 Apostolou Varnava Str.
....22 43 25 77

Makarios III Cultural Centre - The
Archbishopric 22 43 00 08

Holy Monastery of Kykkos Research
Centre, Archangelos Michael Monastery -
south of Nicosia 22 37 00 02

Severios Library - Arch. Kyprianos Square
....22 34 48 88

distances

distances from Nicosia to:

	kms	miles
Limassol..................	86	54
Paphos	149	93
Polis....................	176	109
Troodos	71	44
Larnaka..................	45	28
Ayia Napa.................	80	50
Paralimni/Protaras.......	83	53
Larnaka Airport..........	50	32
Paphos Airport.............	142	88

*A colourful open-air market of fruit
and vegetable in Nicosia*

occupied nicosia-old city
the monuments

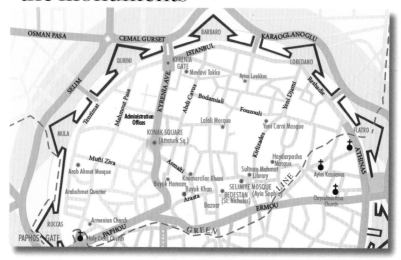

RECENT relaxation in movement across the Green Line between the two communities has made it easier for visitors to go to the Republic's resorts and to visit the old medieval monuments of this part of the divided city, mainly for day trips and excursions. At the time of going to press there are three crossing points in Nicosia - Pedestrians from the Ledra Palace hotel, western side and by car at Ayios Dhometios. Also at the end of Ledra Street in the heart of old Nicosia.

The author has not travelled to the occupied areas and has based his information on other previous, well established publications. He also refers to places and monuments with their original, established names and references.

ARAB AHMET MOSQUE - It is in the heart of the restored historical Arab Ahmet neighbourhood. It was built on the remains of a Lusignan church in 1845. The marble interior dates back to Venetian and Lusignan times. There are said to be tombstones from the 14th century under its stone floor.
Salahi Sevket & Mahumet Pasa Str.   Opens irregularly.

ARABAHMET QUARTER - On the western side of the walled city is the old quarter which has been restored and renovated. Some of the old medieval and Ottoman character has been preserved. Added is a cultural centre and theatre, exhibition hall and cafes.

ARMENIAN CHURCH - Situated on the "Green Line" near the Paphos Gate in the Turkish army controlled area, it is generally agreed to be the former Benedictine of Our Lady of Tyre. The church was given the Armenuan comunity in 1570 as thanks to assisting the Ottomans.

Above: A panoramic view of Old Nicosia from the Ledra Observation. To the front is to be seen Phaneromeni Church, dominant in the background is Selimye Mosque (Ayia Sophia); Below Left: A stamp showing Beyuk Khan -The Great Inn; Below Right is the Koumarcilar (Khan Gamblers Inn)

BUYUK HAMAM (THE GREAT BATH) - It is believed to be build on the remains of the 14th century church of St George of the Latins. In 1570 the church was sacked by the Turks and the Great Bath constructed within the ruins of the nave. The entrance portal sunk well below pavement level is all that remains of the church and it shows were the street level was in the 14th century. In the large domed room you enter from the streeet, a huge nail high above floor level marks the height reached by the 1330 flood of the river Pedieos, in which 3,000 people drowned.

KOUMARCILAR KHANI (THE GAMBLER'S INN) - A 17th century structure, around 50 metres away to the north east of the **Great Inn (Buyuk Khan),** on Asmaalti Square. The courtyard is surrounded by solid arches on the ground floor and above with a verandah which is supported by other columns. A delightful two storey old Inn.

Asma Alti Street   - View the courtyard during daylight - It is privately owned

147

THE BEDESTAN (ST. NICHOLAS CHURCH) - Originally the church of St Nicholas, it was built in the 12th century and after several changes it was given by the Venetians to the Greeks and became the Greek Orthodox Cathedral of Panayia Hodegetria.

After the occupation of Nicosia by the Ottomans, the church remained untouched. In later years however, it was abandoned, fell into neglected and was eventually turned into a covered market (Bedestan) mainly for textiles and other goods. The masonry on the northern entrance resembles that of Ayia Sophia Cathedral. The structure is being restored.

Chapter House is to the east of the Bedestan - a medieval building, perhaps the Chapter House of the Cathedral Church of St Nicholas. There is a collection of fine Coats of Arms and inscribed stones to be seen.

SELIMIYE MOSQUE (CATHEDRAL OF AYIA SOPHIA) - One of the most prominent Frankish monuments in the Eastern Mediterranean. The Cathedral of Ayia Sophia was built in 1193 but the main structure dates to 1209 and is based on the Gothic Cathedrals of France. It was consecrated in 1326 but was never completely finished. It was damaged twice, by the Genoese in 1373 and by the Mameluke Arabs in 1426.

This was a formidable Cathedral where the Lusignans crowned their Kings of Cyprus. The carved windows above the entrance are unequalled examples of Gothic Art. The original Frankish interior was of great splendour with the richness of polished marble, great paintings, silk tapestries and precious metals.

On the 9th of September 1570 the Venetian Bishop of Paphos, Contarini, gave the last sermon while the Ottoman forces besieged the city which was captured shortly afterwards. The Cathedral was then stripped of all remnants of Christianity, all walls were whitewashed and a pair of tall minarets were erected. In 1954 it was renamed as "Selimiye" in honour of the Sultan Selim 2nd. Selimiye Street. Open daily during daylight, but not during prayers.

SULTAN MAHMUT II LIBRARY - Built in 1829 by Sultan Mahmut the 2nd, in the traditional Ottoman architectural style of a single domed chamber with an arched porch, the Library contains a primarily large selection of Turkish books and a fine collection of Korans and manuscripts.

LAPIDARY MUSEUM - A two storey 15th century Venetian House, with fine gothic windows incorporating the coat of arms of the Royal Lusignan Kings, it now serves as a museum.

Among the various relics, one can see the 14th century marble sarcophagus of the Dampierre family.

HAYDAR PASHA MOSQUE (ST KATHERINE CHURCH) - Dated to the 14th century, this is a splendid example of Gothic architecture described as *"the perfect and most elegant in the island."* It has retained a beautiful interior in good condition.

Converted to a mosque in 1570, it now houses an art gallery and an art collection. To the north of Selimiye Mosque, Kirlizade Street. Open: Mon-Sat.

Above: The interior of Selimiye Mosque (the old Latin Ayia Sophia Cathedral); Right; an old view of the monument; Below: A view of the Monument as it dominates the skyline

An old picture of the front doorway of the Bedestan

149

Above: Konak square as seen in this 1950's photograph; Left: Kyrenia Gate as it was; Below: Dervishes as used to perform at Mevlevi Tekke and the building as seen in an old picture

YENI CAMI MOSQUE (THE NEW MOSQUE) - the former Ayios Loukas church., The original structure was built in the 14th century and later was converted to a mosque. It was destroyed in 1772 by the then governor in his belief that he could discover hidden medieval treasures. He failed to do so and even though he built a New Mosque out of remorse, he was beheaded as punishment on the orders of the Sultan.

KONAK SQUARE (SARAY SQUARE) and **VENETIAN COLUMN** - This sector was renamed as *Attaturk Square* and it is the commercial hub of the area and the most important square of the walled city. For centuries it was the centre of government in the island as far back as the Lusignan Kings.
Their Gothic palaces and fine buildings, were all concentrated around this locality and continued to exist and function until a *"an act of vandalism"* carried out by a British administrator in 1904 when the whole area was demolished and 700 years of architecture and history were lost.
The only surviving place is the Hexagonal Fountain. The new buildings were erected to serve the British administrative needs. In the middle of the square is the Venetian Column, a granite pillar believed to have come from the site of ancient Salamis. St.Marks Lion of Venice dominated the top but was then replaced with a sphere made of bronze. This landmark column was moved away by the Turks in 1570 but was erected again by the British in 1917.

MEVLEVI TEKKE (DANCING DERVISHES) - This Tekke, was constructed to honour the **Whirling Dervishes**, who in the 17th century used it as a meeting house for religious music and whirling. Now it is a museum of ethnography and retains its original wooden floor. Also to be seen is the Mausoleum of the Mevlevi Sheikhs - a long row of domed tombs with white turbaned headstones. To the south and very close of Kyrenia Gate. Open: Daily

THE DERVISHES - Semazen
The Semazen (with a camel's - felt hat representing a tombstone and a wide white skirt symbolizing the dead shroud), upon removing his black cloth, is spiritually born to Truth. The Semazens stand with their arms crossed, ready to begin their turn. In their erect posture, they represent the number one, testifying to God's unity. Each rotation takes them past the sheikh, who stands on a red sheep skin. This is a place of Mevlana Celaleddin-i-Rumi, and the sheikh is understood to be a channel for divine grace.
At the start of each of the four movements of the ceremony, the Semazens bow to each other honouring the spirit witin. As their arms unfold, the right hand opens to the skies in prayer, ready to receive God's beneficence. The left hand, upon which his gaze rests, is turned towards the earth in the gesture of bestowal. Fix-footed, he provides a point of contact with this Earth trhough which the divine blessing can flow. Turning from right to left, he embraces all creation as he chants the name of God within the heart.

KYRENIA GATE (PORTA DEL PROVEDITORE) - See also in Nicosia under *Monuments, page 128*. The third of the three Gates that surrounded the City Walls, was restored in 1821 and a domed room was added. It was the formidable exit to the northern part of the island and the castles of the Kyrenia range. In 1931 the British administration widened part of the area to allow the movement of traffic and the Gate now stands in the middle of the road.

LUSIGNAN HOUSE - A 15th century Mansion situated within the ramparts. Its Gothic Arch entrance door, its Lusignan coat of arms, the added Ottoman "Kosk' and the decorated wooden ceilings, make it an interesting sight.

monuments / places of interest in occupied part of Cyprus

Due to the relaxation in movement between the two communities and with both locals and visitors to the island allowed to the northern occupied areas from the south from the various crossing points, we feel that we ought to list some of the old and ancient sites and other places of general interest. The current points of entry at the time of going to press are:

Nicosia - pedestrians by Ledra Palace Hotel
- by car from Ayios Dometios
West of Nicosia - by Pergamos and Strovillia
East of Nicosia - by Zodhia village
Plans are under way to open another two crossings, that of Limnitis in the western area and Athienou area of Larnaka.

The author has not visited any of the areas detailed below but has used information to describe places and monuments from well established and respected publications. The names used are those from before the 1974 occupation, as used officially from the days of the British administration.

Nicosia district

THE TOWN OF MORPHOU

Morphou used to be called the *"Garden of Mesaoria"*. Once it was a proud agricultural centre surrounded by orange groves.
Its Greek population became refugees after the 1974 invasion and occupation by the Turkish army.

Ayios Mamas Church and Monastery - A Franco-Byzantine domed basilica with strong Gothic influence. The only monastic complex in the occupied area that remains intact and has not been desecrated.
Once it was a bustling monastery. No monks reside there now but it is protected by the authorities and occasionally opens for services.
Part of the old Bishop's Palace (residence), situated next to the church has now been converted to a museum of archaeology and natural history. Open Daily

Holy Bishopric of Morphou
Due to the Turkish army occupation of the town, the Bishop of Morphou is temporarily based at Evrychou village, north of Troodos at Solea Valley; Tel: 22 93 24 01

Guzelyurt Museum (Archaeology and Nature Museum) - The most interesting find in the museum is the *Efes Artemis* sculpture found near Salamis

TOUMBA TOU SKOUROU - 3kms to the north of Morphou, this is the ancient site of the area, dating to the bronze age BC although not much is left to be seen.

Above Top: Ayios Mamas church in Morphou shortly after the invasion of 1974 ;
Above: Vouni Palace with its commanding views, another old picture.

VOUNI PALACE -

Situated a few kms to the west of Soloi, along the coast in a commanding position overlooking the sea. This is a unique ancient site, with 137 rooms, built on a hilltop by a pro-Persian Phoenician King in order to keep watch over the Greek city of Soloi near by. *A Royal Residence* that was used during the 5th century BC and had a mixture of Greek (Hellenistic) and Oriental elements.

Its unique position provides spectacular views of the coastline. The wealthy finds of bronze and silver coins, bracelets and numerous gold items are mainly on display at the Cyprus Museum.

Open Daily

Soloi Theatre as was restored and used for performances during the 1960's

SOLOI ANCIENT SITE -

This was one of the original kingdoms of Cyprus. Its name originated from the great Greek philosopher *Solon*. It was built by King Chikokyprios in 580BC and was established as a Greek City Kingdom.

It flourished under the Romans. Temples and a Roman Theatre (dated to 2nd century AD), were found here. The theatre, as seen at present, was completely re-constructed on a nearby site in the 1930's.

During the time of Byzantine Cyprus, Soloi was the Seat of one of the 14 Orthodox Bishops. Later the Orthodox Bishop of Nicosia was exiled here by the Latins.

Most of the old buildings including the Byzantine Cathedral, were knocked down by the mining exploration company in the 1930's and 1940's.

THE BAY OF MORPHOU -

The surrounding areas of Lefka and Karavostasi were known as mining centres even though their history goes back into the mists of time.

Lefka was the rich residential area of the middle ages, then it was taken over by the Turkish settlers after 1571 and the British administration also used it as a mining centre. It retains most of its old traditional architecture.

Karavostasi was famed for its copper mines from ancient times till the 1970's. Due to these mines, the sea near the coast used to be reddish in colour.

KYTHREA AND AREA

15kms to the north east of Nicosia and to the southern slopes of the Kyrenia mountain range. Kythrea was famous for its romantic folklore and idyllic surroundings. The centre of attraction was **Kephalovryso Spring** - *(the head fountain spring)* situated amongst greenery and lavish vegetation. Due to its position, its continuously flowing springs, it became an important centre throughout the centuries.

Pre 1974, the people of Nicosia used to travel there for relaxing weekends. It was also here that the famous bronze statue of the Roman Emperor Septimius Severus was found in the nearby site of **Chytri**. The life-size statue is one of the main attractions in the Cyprus Museum in Nicosia.

154

Kyrenia town and district

Once it was the Jewel of the Eastern Mediterranean. It was the most idyllic and romantic place in the whole of the Eastern Mediterranean with its picturesque horse shoe shaped harbour, known as the St Tropez of the East.

Kyrenia was an ancient Kingdom City but there is not much remaining of that period. It is the Seat of one of the four Bishops of the island, now exiled. In medieval times it was a port with fortifications surrounding the town, and dominated by the Royal Castle.

Places below have been given their traditional names.

Kyrenia town

HOLY BISHOPRIC OF KYRENIA

Since the occupation of the Turkish army the Holy Bishop is temporarily based in Nicosia free part at: 3 Achilleos Street, Angladjia Tel: 22 44 42 42

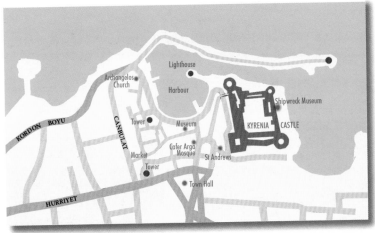

KYRENIA CASTLE -

This is one of the best surviving medieval architectural treasures of the island and it dominates the harbour. Built in 1211 by Jean d' Ibelin during the reign of Hugh I, it was used as a Royal Residence by Alix de Champagne.

In a siege by the Genoese in 1374, the castle suffered extensive damage. Later, Venetian additions destroyed part of the original structure. The new building was the west wall and the towers to the northwest and southeast. The bridge which replaced the original drawbridge leads into the castle.

The small Byzantine chapel is the only remaining pre-Lusignan/Venetian structure. Also surviving is the original gate with the Lusignan coat of arms. The Castle also retains some of the massive structures of medieval buildings and the Royal Apartments. Situated by the seafront.   Open Daily

SHIPWRECK MUSEUM - Situated within the Castle area, this is a preserved cargo ship discovered in the 1960's by a local diver and dated to around 300BC. The boat, some 14 metres long, with a cargo of wine, almonds and mill stones, also with pots and amphora was rescued and carefully reconstructed by local archaeologists and a special team from Pennsylvania University in the USA.

THE HARBOUR -

This was once a neglected, small fishing harbour, enlarged by the British administration in 1891 and the warehouses built were for the main trade of citrus and carobs.

In the 1960's and 1970's it took a more cosmopolitan look, until the 1974 invation and the subsequent uprooting of all the Greek inhabitants.

ARCHANGELOS CHURCH - now an Icon Museum, this church built in 1860 with its bell tower, used to dominate every postcard of Kyrenia Harbour. After it was abandoned in 1974, it was converted into a Byzantine Icon Museum. Its original iconostasi was saved and retained. Other icons were brought here from numerous abandoned churches for safe keeping away from looters. Thus, this surreal icon museum was established.   Open Daily

ROMAN CATHOLIC CHURCH OF ST. ELIZABETH - The church was built by Major Tankerville Chamberlayne who was a commissioner of Kyrenia 1914-18. Its walls incorporated older medieval structures.

FOLK ART MUSEUM - This small collection is housed in an 18th century period building, situated behind the harbour. It contains embroidery, kitchen tools and other artifacts.   Open   Mon-Fri

Left: The Castle as seen in this old postage stamp
Right: The Pentadaktilos peak from an old photograph.

Above: The Abbey of Bellapais (the Abbey of Peace)...Below: One of the plates of Lamboussa treasures, now at the Nicosia Museum; Right: Formidable St Hilarion Castle; Below Bottom: The monastery of Ayios Ioannis Chrysostomos as it was before the invasion (see p157)

narrow buildings. It is an amazing place, a fascinating medieval castle with a rich history which has inspired poets and writers over the centuries. In 1228 it experienced a bloody two year siege by the representatives of the German Emperor Frederick II on his way to Palestine. They eventually captured it and it remained in their hands till 1232 when it was recaptured by King Henry I after ambushing the garrison in June.

LAPITHOS AREA - For years it established itself as an important place of great beauty and in by-gone days attracted weekend visitors from Nicosia, who went to see the famous *Spring of Kefalovryso* - a place of romance and poetry.

LAMBOUSA - is to the west of Lapithos and Karavas, along the coast. Lambousa was also known as *Lapethos*, an ancient Greek colony and one of the Kingdoms of the island, it was founded by Praxandros. In the Byzantine period and till 1222 it was one of the Seats of Bishops. The area now is believed to be out of bounds.

The Lambousa Collection -

This is a rare collection of Silver Plates, Golden Medallions and Necklaces that were found here in 1902 and are now on display at Cyprus Museum. Others are in the British Museum and New York Metropolitan Museum.

ACHIROPIITOS MONASTERY - situated next to the ruins of ancient Lambousa which were incorporated in the monastic structures. The church is impressive, a cruciform dome building with a porch dating back to the Frankish period. It was sacked in 1765 by mainland Turks and was further destroyed in 1821. Most of the monks were put to death. Thus its decline began.

This is currently a controlled area under the Turkish army and is out of bounds to visitors.

MYRTOU VILLAGE AREA - here are: *Ayios Panteleimon Church* - believed to have been built around 1735 as a church, then extended with some living quarters.

Pigadhes Site - Near the Myrtou village is this ancient Bronze Age site. Still visible amongst the ruins is the double horned, 12 foot high altar and surrounding remaining buildings.

KORMAKITIS AREA (Peninsular) - about 25kms from the western corner of Kyrenia, The journey along the coast, it makes for a spectacular drive by the cliffs and the sea.

Kormakitis Village - It retains a small Maronite Christian community and a functioning church.

Ayia Irene - There is an old chapel outside the village near a ravine where there were finds of pygmy hippos.

Paleokastro - An ancient settlement with remains of a Temple. An important discovery was made here of hundreds of terracotta figures of different sizes, now on display at the Cyprus Museum.

Famagusta town, district and Karpasia
Famagusta Old Town

For centuries it was the most sophisticated and important city in the island and a major port trading with the Levant. The original capital was **Salamis,** further to the north, which was sacked by the Arabs in 648AD

Today's Famagusta originated from a small 3rd century BC settlement, but it started taking real shape in 1291 after the fall of Acre in the Levant, when many Christian refugees came here to settle. Soon afterwards it started growing and flourished. Soon its natural harbour became a major trading centre in the Medieval Eastern Mediterranean.

Between 1372-1464 it was under the control of the Genoese and in 1481-1571 under the Venetians who strengthened its fortifications. The famous long siege which lasted for 13 months ended in 1571 with the Ottoman Turks eventually capturing the ruined city. The new rulers forbade all Christians within the perimeter of the City Walls. Thus, the surviving Greek population started moving to the south and a new town was established called **Varoshia.**

In the 1960s and 1970s it experienced amazing growth and was crowned as the *Riviera of the East* due to its fine sandy beaches and cosmopolitan atmosphere. The 1974 Turkish invasion put an end to all that. The Greek inhabitants abandoned their homes as refugees and since then the place has become a ghost town. Here again we list the most important places with their original names as they were known for many years.

THE LAND GATE - One one of the two main gates entering the City - at the south western corner - about 30 feet high, built with great engineering skills during the Lusignan period.

The out-work protection, was added by the Venetians in 1544. The new gate entering the City is next to the old one.

THE SEA GATE - It connected the city with the sea to the east. It was built by the Venetian captain Nicola Prioli in 1496. whose coat of arms is visible together with the **Venetian Lion** above the Gate. It joined the City and the Harbour - a fine and great example of Venetian defence Architecture.

Old picture of Famagusta Harbour, the City Walls and dominant the Cathedral of St Nicholas, now Lala Mustafa Pasa Mosque

161

TER AND ST PAUL church now **Sinan Pasa Mosque** - Once an
Jox church it was built at the end of the 14th century by merchant
Simon Nostrano. Later it was converted and used as a mosque and was
recently renovated. It is now used as a Cultural venue for exhibitions, concerts and theatre, it was also as a public library.

It was a very strong and impressive structure, similar in style to the architecture of southern France but with some local characteristics and an interior of columns and arches.

PALAZZO DEL PROVEDIORE - The Grand Palace of the Venetian Governors.
The only surviving part of the structure is an arched portico with four large
granite columns which were moved from Salamis.
The most impressive part of the remains is the outer facade with it's three
arches. The Revier coat of arms is to be seen above the arches. On the southern side of the courtyard are the remnants of the Palace and the Venetian
armoury. The place is open during daylight

ST GEORGE OF THE GREEKS - Built in the 14th century on the burial site of
the first Archbishop of Cyprus Epifanios of Constantia (310-404) - His remains were later moved to Constantinople in 900 by Emperor Leo.
It is thought to have been modelled on the St. Chapelle Church in Paris and
this mixture of Byzantine and Gothic styles was destroyed during the siege in
1571. Now, a roofless ruin, a shadow of its old glory, it is situated in the southern part of Medieval Famagusta. This remained for some time after the
conquest as a Greek quarter and other Orthodox churches also existed such
as Ayios Simeon, and Ayia Zoni.

The ruins of St George of the Greeks (C. Russell)

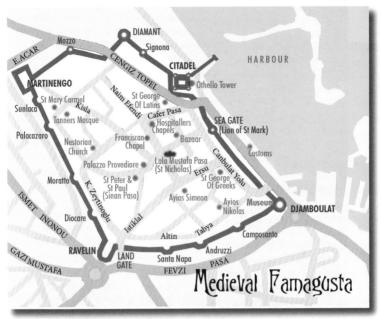

Medieval Famagusta

DIAMANT
Mozzo
Signona
E.ACAR
CENGIZ TOPEL
CITADEL
MARTINENGO
Othello Tower
HARBOUR
St George Of Latins
St Mary Carmel
Kisla
Naim Efendi
Cafer Pasa
SEA GATE
(Lion of St Mark)
Sunlaca
Tanners Mosque
Hospitallers
Chapels
Palacazaro
Nestorian Church
Franciscan Chapel
Bazaar
Customs
Lala Mustafa Pasa
(St Nicholas)
Canbulat Yolu
Palazzo Provediore
Ersu
St George Of Greeks
Moratto
K. Zeytinoglu
St Peter & St Paul
(Sinan Pasa)
Ayios Simeon
Ayios Nikolas
Museum
DJAMBOULAT
ISMET INONOU
Diocare
Istiklal
Altin
Tabya
Camposanto
GAZI MUSTAFA
RAVELIN
LAND GATE
Santa Napa
FEVZI
Andruzzi
PASA

Top: Map with monuments within the walled city of Famagusta
Above and Left: Two views of the surviving formidable Venetian Walls
(left: C. Russell)

163

Above: Lala Mustafa Pasa Mosque (the Latin Cathedral of St Nicholas), a fine example of gothic splendour; Below Left: A 1950's view of the famous Othello Tower with the Lion of Venice; Below Right: The ruins of St George of the Latins (colour photos, C.Russell)

164

LALA MUSTAFA PASA MOSQUE - (CATHEDRAL OF ST.NICHOLAS)

The former Latin Cathedral of Saint Nicholas, it was turned into a mosque after the capture of the City in 1571 and was built in 1308 by the 5th Latin Bishop Baldwin Lambert. It is a great example of 14th century French Gothic grandeur and is of a similar plan to that of the Rheims Cathedral. Untill the capture of the City by the Genoese in 1372, the Lusignan Kings of Cyprus were crowned here as *"Kings of Jerusalem"*.

Two granite columns from an ancient tomb were erected by the Venetians and are incorporated into the walls. During the great siege some damage occurred but the structure survived along with the western facade with its 3 moulded grand doorways. All the richness of its Latin interior were removed by the Ottoman conquerors and changed to a simplistic and empty presence. Visitors can visit during prayer hours on a daily basis - Entrance: Free

THE BAZAAR (MARKET)-Naim Effendi Sokaki
This area was once the main mercantile district of Medieval Famagusta, full of splendour, richness and life. Now, it is the main market place, situated just to the north of Lala Mustafa Pasa Mosque.
It has courtyards and arches and is surrounded by medieval buildings such as the 15th century *Biddulph Gate* and the *Cellar of St Claire Convent.*

OTHELLO TOWER - THE CITADEL
Built in the 14th century, this square castle (citadel) is one of the best remembered and few surviving elements of the Lusignan period. Its main objective was to defend the port.   It was renovated by the Venetian captain Nicolo Foscarini Oscareno in 1492.
The Great Hall is very interesting. The main characteristic of the entrance is the large winged *Lion of Venice* plaque above the arched gate. It is thought that when Leonardo da Vinci visited Cyprus in 1481, he advised the Venetians on the design of the defenses of Famagusta. This is named the *Othello Tower* after the play by Shakespeare, based on events which occurred in the castle.
From the top of the citadel battlements, one can enjoy panoramic views of the old town and harbour.
Open regularly - during daytime

ST. GEORGE OF THE LATINE - Situated opposite the citadel (Othello's Tower), it is one of the best examples of an early Gothic Style church, dating to the 13th century. It was built by masons brought over from the Rhineland in Germany. Most of the building is in ruins and roofless, with only two walls standing, the vaulting and sacristy remain.

TWIN CHURCHES (Hospitallers Chapels) - Situated near the ruins of St. Francis these twin churches are believed to be those of the Crusader Orders of **The Templars** and **Hospitallers.** The largest of the structures being of *St. Anthony* of the Knights Templar order, built in 1300. The smaller chapel of the Knights Hospitallers was added in 1308. The buildings have been renovated and currently house a cultural centre and an art gallery.

ST. FRANCIS CHURCH (FRANCISCAN CHAPEL) - Situated to the north of the Venetian Palace, this was an extensive convent, built by King Henry II (1285-1324) and only parts of it have survived, such as the chapel and a small part of the church. There are also some tombstones of merchants, nobles of French , Genoese and Venetian origins. Next to it the Turks built a Turkish Bath (Hamman) and an aqueduct. It now houses a discotheque.

NESTORIAN CHURCH - Built in the middle of the 14th century by Sir Francis Lakhas, a very wealthy merchant. This was a great church of the Nestorian sect of the Assyrian Patriarch's representatives, a Christian-Syrian sect. It was covered with murals and inscriptions and later become a Greek Orthodox church named Ayios Georgios O Xorinos (The Exile). The rich interior has now gone. It is occasionally open and used for cultural events.

Other Frankish period Churches were: **Ayia Anna** - most of it survives including mural paintings. **St. Mary Carmel** - Carmelite church, once a monastery of St. Mary of Carmel, only some structures remain. An **Armenian Church** - most of it survived and includes some wall paintings and Armenian inscriptions.

MARTINENGO BASTION - With magnificent architecture, this massive engineering achievement was built by the Venetian Giovanni Girolamo 1550-59. It was not damaged during the long siege and most of it survived. The interior also provides an indication of the perfection and masters of the Venetian experts.

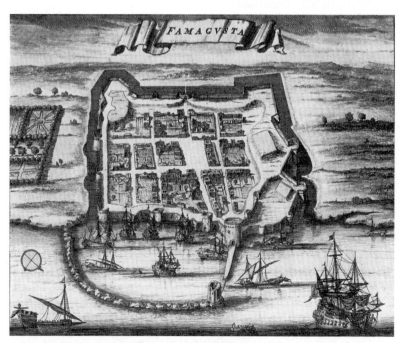

A medieval map engraving of Famagusta and its fortifications

Famagusta district and Karpasia

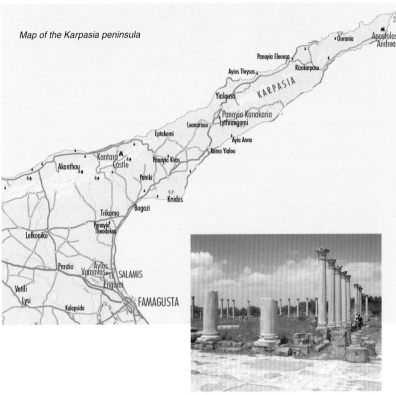

Map of the Karpasia peninsula

A recent photograph of the ruins of ancient Salamis (C.Russell)

ANCIENT CITY OF SALAMIS

8kms to the north of Famagusta

One of the most important ancient cities of the Mediterranean.

Founded around the 12th century BC by the Greek hero of the Trojan War, *Teucer (Tefkros)*, the son of Telemachos, King of Salamis in Greece. The Greek culture, way of life and language were the dominant characteristics of this city in contrast to other city-kingdoms who were under the influence of the Phoenician merchants or colonised by Persians, Assyrians and Egyptians.

Natural and man made catastrophes and the Jewish Revolt in 115-117 AD brought much destruction to the place as did the earthquakes of the early 4th century AD. It was rebuilt in 337-361 by Emperor Constantine and called **Constantia**. It had its final "death blow" in 648 after several destructive Arab raids. With Christianity emerging as the New Order after the Romans, the city had one of the greatest prelates in the island, its Bishop *Epifanius* (368-404). During his time, the largest cathedral of its kind was built here.

167

Salamis coins ; Left: First gold coin issued by Evagoras 1st 411-373BC; Right: A gold stater from Salamis, issued by Evagoras 2nd, c.361-351BC

EVAGORAS

Most famous of all its Kings was EVAGORAS I who reigned 410-374 BC. He fought the Persian rulers during a long campaign and despite his defeat, he retained his throne and paid tributes to the Persian king Artarxerxes.

The greatest ruler in the island, he supported the Arts and Commerce and erected great buildings in Salamis.

He established a centre of Greek Culture and Athenian and other Orators and artisans were regular visitors.

The site of Salamis

It was excavated at various times by Cypriot and International Archaeologists, the most recent being the *"Father of Cyprus Archaeology"* Dr Vasos Karayiorgis who's work ended abruptly after the Turkish invasion and occupation of the area in 1974. Before that date, parts of the site had been reconstructed, such as the impressive theatre which was a cultural centre for various performances of ancient Greek Plays in the 1960's.   Open Daily

The Theatre - Built by the Romans during the time of the Emperor Augustus and based on Hellenistic style, it was estimated to seat over 2000 spectators. When excavations started, it was practically buried in sand. It is the largest ancient theatre discovered in the island.

Gymnasium / Forum - This is the most important of the finds, part were originally excavated in 1890 and the work continued up to 1974. A wealth of discoveries were made including statues, gold coins, excellent pottery and inscriptions. Many of them are displayed in the Cyprus Museum.

Some of the marble columns were restored and many re-erected but since 1974 not much has happened.

GYMNASIA were the educational and cultural centres as well as recreational. High levels of physical training was of great importance - **"all for a healthy body and healthy mind"**.....

Within the complex are: The Palaestra - an open air gymnasium and centre for contests and other activities. **The Baths** - to the eastern side of the complex with hot rooms, passages and halls.

The Roman Villa - Close to the road, south of the main city of Salamis, a once large Roman Villa. The foundations reveal stone floors and living rooms around a courtyard.

168

The Ancient
Greek Kingdom - City
of Salamis

Left: Location map of the site of ancient Salamis; Above: A stamp with the ruins of Salamis; Below: A 1960's photo of the ancient site as restored by the father of Cyprus archaeology Dr Vasos Karayiorgis and Cyprus Museum

The Basilica - Known as *Kampanopetra,* near the Roman Villa and close to the sea, this is one of the earliest Basilicas in the island, built in the 4th century AD it was perhaps the biggest complex on the island.

Ayios Epifanios Cathedral - Some 300 metres to the south of the Theatre. It was an impressive, large structure built by St. Epifanios, the bishop of Constantia around 380 AD.

The Water Cistern - To the south of the Cathedral, this must have been a very important Cistern, water complex. The aqueduct brought water from Kythrea, some 25 miles to the northwest.
Around here was also the Marketplace-Agora of the City.

169

PRISON OF ST KATHERINE

This site is located between Salamis and St.Barnabas monastery. It is of a Graeco-Roman origin, an unusual megalithic structure where, according to local legend, St. Katherine was imprisoned around the end of the 3rd century AD, before she was transferred to Alexandria for her martyrdom.

ROYAL TOMBS

This group of around 6 tombs dates to the 8th century BC. They are the most important of many such tombs which are scattered around the area. Excavations carried out in the 1960's by Dr. Karayiorgis and despite the fact that some had previously been looted, the finds were spectacular. Many of the items are now in the Cyprus Museum. A small museum was recently erected at the site which incorporates the preserved tombs.
Open Daily

ENGOMI ANCIENT SITE

The remains of this important ancient city are to the south of St Barnabas monastery, the Bronze Age City of *Engomi*, also known as *Alasia*. Most of its ruins are buried in silt. A wealth of treasures were uncovered here, some are now at the Cyprus museum - including the famous *"Horned God"* statue. Others are in the British Museum.

It flourished for around 700 years, from 1800 to 1050 BC when it was finally destroyed and abandoned. During those years it was an important centre for the smelting and exporting of Copper, a precious commodity and a major export of Cyprus in those days.
Sadly, after the 1974 invasion, the site was neglected and left to the elements.

ST BARNABAS (also Ayios Varnavas) MONASTERY

First built between the 5th and 6th centuries AD and financed by Emperor Zeno to commemorate the miraculous discovery of the body of the Saint in this spot.
After the act, the Emperor granted Independence to the Church of Cyprus - *Autokefalos* and it became free to have its own Archbishop.
Barnabas was a native of Salamis, he brought the Gospel to the island and together with Apostles Paul and Mark pioneered the spread of Christianity in the island. The actual structure of the church underwent later additions. It is a Byzantine domed church, it is believed that originally it was larger with a third dome.

The church and the monastic complex expanded in the 1950's and 1960's, when it became a centre for icon painting and its teaching. Students and worshippers visited the place regularly.
Celebration date is June 11th

The last monks were forced to leave by the occupying authorities in 1976. They then converted the gatehouse and monastic buildings into a museum displaying icons from the churches and archaeological finds from the surrounding area.   Open Daily

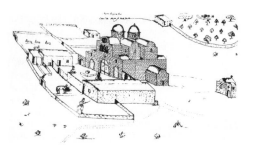

The Monastery of Apostolos Barnabas; Right: a drawing by Barsky during his travels; Below: The monastery as seen in recent times and used by the occupied authorities as museum. (C.Russell)

Engomi ancient site: Left: as seen in an old photograph; Above: A clay tablet found in the site with the strange cypro-minoan script (Cyprus Museum)

171

LYSI VILLAGE / Ayios Epifanios Church

This and the surrounding areas of **Mesaoria plateau** were one of the main agricultural centres - a traditional example of bygone Cypriot rural life. Its Greek inhabitants are now refugees. Rich in agriculture but also rich with its ancient, Byzantine and medieval past

Ayios Epifanios - is the most important church of the area, 2kms south of Lysi. It contained wonderful frescos, stolen, then discovered in Texas USA where the American court ordered their safe return to the island once a permanent political solution is reached.

TREMETHOUSIA VILLAGE / Ayios Spyridon Church

Another important agricultural centre, full of history and rural traditions. The Roman city ruins are out of bounds.

Ayios Spyridon Church - was built on the foundations of a very early Christian church. It was a centre for the restoration of icons.

It had an impressive collection of these and an iconostasi which was sadly removed after the occupation.

Celebrates: 12th December

TRIKOMO VILLAGE / Panayia Theodokos Church

Another important rural village with lots of traditions and past memories, now emptied of its Greek inhabitants.

Panayia Theodokos Church - this one was saved by the occupying authorities and turned into a museum of Byzantine icons. It was a 12th century chapel, enlarged in the 15th century. A bell tower was added in the 19th century. The interior of the church has some powerful and well executed murals. The icon museum opens daily

AKANTHOU VILLAGE / Panayia Pergaminitissa

Once a very important agricultural centre, its original inhabitants are now refugees.

Panayia Pergaminitissa - also known as The Lady of Pergamon church is 4kms to the north of Akanthou. Originally it was a large 5th. century church, visited by many pilgrims in the past. It has now been abandoned and its icons and frescos removed.

BOGAZI / Knidos ancient site

Situated on the southern coast of the Karpas peninsular (the finger further east). This sandy beach and beautiful coastline were, before the invasion, the excursion spots of the young set from Varoshia. It was also a major stopping place for pilgrims en route to Apostolos Andreas Monastery.

It is still a major tourist attraction with fish restaurants and has undergone major development.

Knidos - Near Bogazi, is the site of an ancient Phoenician trading settlement and a place where many wrecks of old vessels are strewn along the coast.

KANTARA CASTLE

12kms north of Bogazi - 2,063 feet height

The third of the major castles of the Kyrenia range, on the eastern side, it boasts the best views of the three.   It was of great strategic importance, being impregnable due to the surrounding steep precipices. Dates to around 1300 AD and it is a mixture of natural and man made defenses.

A spectacular castle, with some sections still intact, it is probably the best preserved. other part of which is in ruins, but also is full of fantasies and imagination. This combines with its beautiful natural surroundings and the fascinating lights and colours observed from the top.

From here one can see the northern coast as well as the Famagust harbour.

Open Daily

Panoramic view from Kantara Castle (C. Russell)

Two views of bygone years from the Mesaoria plains, rich in agriculture and and traditional rural life...

LYTHRANGOMI VILLAGE / Panayia Kanakaria

An old and well known village of the Karpas area, once full of tradition. It is an agricultural centre whose Greek inhabitants were driven out in 1974.

Panayia Kanakaria - one of the best known churches in the island, a 12th century domed structure with some later additions. It suffered damage and extensive looting after the invasion and one of its treasured mosaics, that of *Virgin Mary* from around 500 AD was offered to the Getty Museum USA. After legal action by the Cyprus Government, the American courts returned it to the island and it is now on show at the Byzantine Museum in Nicosia.

YIALOUSA / Ayia Trias Church

This is another well known traditional village of the Karpasia peninsula. **Ayia Trias Church** - is situated to the east of Yialousa village. The original church dates to around the 6th century as do the Baptistry and town streets and blocks of the early village. Remains of the church include the Hall, Mosaic floors and other buildings such as the Bishop's residence.

RIZOKARPASO VILLAGE / Churches

This is the last village on the far eastern side of Karpasia It is an important agricultural centre which suffered depopulation after the 1974 invasion. However, a small and determined number of Greek Cypriots remained here, living under pressure in a small enclave. In ancient times, it was the site of ancient **Carpasia** and some ruins can be seen by the seashore.

Cathedral of Ayios Synesios - this is used by the local Greek community. It was once a much larger church, a Cathedral, serving the Orthodox Bishop of Famagusta when the Latins expelled him here.

Ayios Philon Church - a cruciform domed church, built in the 10th century on the foundations of an earlier church. It is of a Romanesque (Norman) style, only found in the Karpas area and is situated to the north of the village, close to the sea. Some of the mosaic floors have survived.

CAPE APOSTOLOS ANDREAS

To the eastern end of the monastery, is the point where Cyprus land ends. It is a rocky landscape and seascape with coves, rocks, coastal mist, a truly mystical place....On a clear day, the Syrian coast is visible in the distance.

Here, one of the oldest villages in the island, which dates to the early Neolithic period, was discovered in the location of *Kastros*, one theory being that it was a fishermen's settlement.

Here also stood the shrine of **Aphrodite Acrea,** which, according to historians, was of a more mysterious and mystical cult than that of Aphrodite in the rest of the island.

APOSTOLOS ANDREAS MONASTERY

The most historical and most popular monastery and religious centre of all Orthodox Cypriots, situated at the far end of this isolated part of the long Karpasia peninsula.

It started as a small chapel on the spot where Apostle Andreas came ashore to preach Christianity. It was expanded over the centuries as a monastic settlement and it was also used for overnight accommodation for the many pilgrims, some from as far away as Paphos. From where, according to type of transport, it used to take 2-3 days to reach. This holy place bears some similarity to Lourdes in France.

The war of 1974, and occupation, the expulsion of the Greek population, forced the monks and keepers to abandon it and it soon went into a state of decay.

In recent years, with the relaxation of movement between the two communities, repairs have been made to the church and some of the buildings. Some monks and keepers have returned and the monastery is coming to life. Once more, some pilgrims adventure the long drive to pray at the monastery. The existing chapel belongs to the 15th century with later additions to the church, bell tower and monastic buildings.

Celebrates: 30th November and 15th August.

Apostolos Andreas, the most Holy of all Monasteries; Left as it was in the pre 1974 occupation and Below, recently, visitors were allowed to return
(Andreas Petrou)

general information

CYPRUS TOURISM ORGANISATION known for short as: CTO

This is the organisation which provides all the information and services related to the Tourist Industry, promotions, publications, all through the Republic of Cyprus. In each resort we list the offices. It is also important to mention that the CTO publishes a number of interesting and colourful booklets such as *Cyprus for Sports, Cyprus for Cycling, Hidden Cyprus, Natural Trails* and others which are available on request.

Head Office - correspondence only   POBox 25535, CY 1390 Lefkosia (Nicosia) Tel: 00 357 22 69 11 00   Fax: 00 357 22 33 16 44   email: cytour@cto.org.cy website: **www.visitcyprus.org.uk**

PUBLIC HOLIDAYS

Listed below are the official public holidays of the Republic. All Public Services, Private Enterprises, Archaeological Sites and Museums and in most cases, Banks and Shops are closed. Many supermarkets and shops remain open in tourist areas.

JANUARY 1st - **New Year's Day**
JANUARY 6th - **Epiphany Day**
FEBRUARY - MARCH - **Green Monday** - Movable
MARCH 25th - **Greek National Day**
APRIL 1st - **Greek Cypriot National Day**
SPRING GREEK EASTER- **Greek Orthodox Easter** - Movable**:**
                        Good Friday; Easter Sunday; Easter Monday
MAY 1st - **Labour Day**
WHITSUN **(Kataklysmos)** - 50 Days after Orthodox Easter
AUGUST 15th - **Assumption Day** -The Day of the Holy Virgin Mary
OCTOBER 1st - **Cyprus Independence Day**
OCTOBER 28th - **Greek National Day**
DECEMBER 25th - **Christmas Day**
DECEMBER 26th - **Boxing Day**

Note: Turkish Cypriots observe other religious and national holidays which are not listed here.

HOW TO ENTER THE REPUBLIC / CUSTOMS

For updated information you may contact either the Cyprus Tourist Office in your country of origin or the High Commission or Embassy of the Republic in your home country

Also please note the following:

- Fly only to the recognised international airports of Larnaka and Paphos.

- Over 40 airlines connect Britain, Europe and the Middle East with services which extend to the rest of the world. Cyprus Airways is the National Carrier.

- By boat through the main recognised ports of Limassol and Larnaka

- Sailing to the two main marinas of Larnaka, managed by the CTO and Limassol
- St. Raphael, a private marina

- Visas: No visas are required for European Community Nationals. Others need to get advice from the consulates and embassies.

- No vaccination is required from EC nationals and most other countries except from any infected countries, when a valid certificate is needed.

- For medical purposes, visitors are advised to carry Medical Insurance. EC nationals should also obtain their special medical form for treatment within the European Community.

- No limit to cheques/travellers cheques or card transactions. Gold and bank notes in excess over Euro12,500 must be declared

- There is no limit as to what one buys or takes between EC countries providing it is for personal use only.

- Importation , possession and use of narcotic drugs and other substances is strictly prohibited and punished by arrest and trial.

- The same applies to weapons, articles presenting a health risk and forgeries.

- Exportation of Antiquities and other cultural heritage articles is strictly prohibited.   see **www.mof.gov.cy**

TRANSPORT

Bus Services- Local and Inter-city; refer to the end of each resort. A regular Bus service between Nicosia and Larnaka Airpot is planned for the near future.
Taxi Services - Travel Express, inter-city connections (shared taxi):
Tel: 22 73 08 88 or 77 77 74 74

AA Cyprus 24 hr Break down Nicosia Tel 22 31 31 31
Cyprus Automobile Association - www.cyprusaa.org
Note: For complaints about drivers or vehicles call: 22 80 71 01/24 82 82 55
between 08-14.00, Mon-Fri or on other times to nearest police: 1460
Notes to Drivers:
Petrol Stations usually close Saturday afternoons, Sundays and Holidays. Most then operate with automatic filling machines by first inserting money... follow instructions

Car Rentals available from airports and all resorts. It usually comes with a full tank
of petrol for
which you pay
extra, partly
refundable on
return otherwise
return nearly
empty.

useful contacts
Calls from abroad start with 00357 then local......

MEDICAL -
European Community Medical form EU-EIII for out-patient and in-patient treatment.
Accident and Emergency treatment is Free.
Pancyprian Medical Association Tel: 22 31 68 12 email:cycma@cytanet.com.cy
Private Clinics & Hospitals Tel: 22 66 51 0 email: info@oeb.org.cy
Cyprus Dental Association Tel: 22 31 68 74 email: info@dental.org.cy

EDUCATIONAL/ MEDIA
University of Cyprus Tel: 22 89 20 00 www.ucy.ac.cy
Press Information Office Tel: 22 80 11 21 www.pio.gov.cy email: pioxx@cytanet.com.cy
Cyprus News Agency Tel: 22 55 61 00 www.cna.org.cy
Cyprus Broadcasting Corporation Tel: 22 42 22 31

CULTURAL COUNCILS in Nicosia
British Council - new premises in the heart of Nicosia: Aristotelous Street
Tel: 22 58 50 00
French Cultural Centre -Metochiou 4, Tel: 22 45 93 33
American Centre - c/o Embassy-Engomi 33B, Tel: 22 39 39 39
Goethe Institute Tel: 22 66 66 14 www.goethecy.org
Russian Cultural Centre - Alasias 16, Nicosia Tel: 22 76 16 07

CONSUMERS / COMMERCE
Consumer Association Tel: 22 51 61 12 www.cyprusconsumers.org.cy
Cyprus Chamber of Commerce & Industry - www.ccci.org.cy
Lost Credit Cards - JCC payment systems Ltd, 16 Stasikratous Str. Nicosia
Tel: 22 86 81 00 (24hrs)
Youth Card "EURO 26" - E.C. service for young people age 13 - 26years, offering
hundreds of discounts on products/services. Valid in total 41 European Countries.
Youth Board of Cyprus: Tel: 22 40 26 14 email: info@youthboard.org.cy
www.youthboard.org.cy
Central Bank of Cyprus email. cbcinfo@centralbank.gov.cy www.centralbank.gov.cy
Ministry of Commerce & Industry www.meit.gov.cy
Ministry of Finance and Investment www.mof.gov.cy

Real Estate Agents Association www.ccci.org.cy www.skek-creaa.com

GENERAL ACTIVITIES / OTHERS
Bird Watching - Cyprus Orthological Society Tel: 22 45 50 72
email: birdlifecy@cytanet.com.cy www.birdlifecyprus.org
Cycling - Cycling Federation: TeL; 22 66 33 44 email: ccf@cytanet.com.cy
Mountain Bike Association: 22 35 61 74; BikeTrek: www.biketreckcyprus.com
Horse Racing - Nicosia Race Club Tel: 22 78 27 27 www.nicosiaraceclub.com.cy-
Horse Riding - Cyprus Equestrian Federation email: notorious.equ@cytanet.com.cy-
Football & Training - Football Federation: Tel: 22 35 23 41
Diving - Federation of Underwater Diving: Tel: 22 75 46 47
Golf - see in resort general information
Shooting - Cyprus Shooting Association: Tel: 22 48 66 73 www.cssfshooting.org
Tennis- Cyprus Tennis Federation : Tel: 22 66 68 22 cytennis@spidernet.com.cy
www.cyprustennis.com
Cruises - along Eastern Mediterranean - Louis Cruises: www.louisecrises.com
-Salamis Tours: www.salamis-tours.com; -Paradise Island : www.paradise.com.cy

Sailing/Yachting/Sighting Tours/Hotel Reservations/ Consulates & Embassies and any
other information needed - Best updates from the CTO Travellers
Handbook, published annually. Ask at your local Tourist Office or
www.visitcyprus.org.cy
Cyprus Sports Organisations email: info@sport-koa.org.cy www.sport-koa.org.cy
Tel: 22 89 70 00
Youth Hostels - Cyprus Youth Hostel Association em: montis@logos.cy.net
Philately Tel: 22 80 57 26 www.mcw.gov.cy/dps
Snow Skiing - Cyprus Ski Club: Tel: 22 67 53 40   www.cyprusski.com
Cyprus Car Rally/Automobile Association   Tel: 22 31 32 33   www.cyprusAA.org
Angling - www.moa.gov.cy/dfmr   dept of Fisheries Tel; 22 80 78 62
Aviation Sports - www.caf.org.cy
Climbing - www.komoa.com
Weddings - Cyprus Municipalities www.ucm.org.cy
Cyprus Agrotourism; c/o CTO 19 Lemesos Avenue, Nicosia Tel: 22 34 00 71

TELEPHONE SERVICES
NATIONAL DIRECTORY - 192
INTERNATIONAL DIRECTORY - 194
INTERNATIONAL CALLS - 198
EXACT TIME *English* -193 *Greek* -195
FAULTS REPORT -197   CUSTOMER CALL CENTRE -132

Airports: LARNAKA INTERNATIONAL-77 77 88 33
PAPHOS INTERNATIONAL- 77 77 88 33

CHEMISTS/PHARMACIES

To out of office hours services (first number in English language, second in Greek)

Nicosia	90 90 14 12	90 90 14 02
Limassol	90 90 14 15	90 90 14 05
Larnaka	90 90 14 14	90 90 14 04
Paphos	90 90 14 16	90 90 14 06
Paralimni	90 90 14 13	90 90 14 03

ARCHAEOLOGICAL SOCIETIES AND CULTURAL FOUNDATIONS

Cyprus Department of Antiquities   antiquitiesdept@da.mcw.gov.cy
www.mcw.gov.cy/da
Cyprus Research Centre Tel: 22 45 63 01
The Association of Cypriot Archaeologists   P.O.Box 20058, 1600 Lefkosia
Cyprus American Archaeological Research Institute www.caari.org
Archaeological Research Unit, University of Cyprus www.ucy.ac.cy/isa G
Anastasios G. Leventis Foundation www.leventisfoundation.org
Bank of Cyprus Cultural Foundation www.boccf.org
Laiki Group Cultural Centre culturalcenter@laiki.com
Pierides Foundation centrart@spidernet.com.cy
Centre of Cultural Heritage   www.heritage.org.cy

For updated full list please ask from the CTO the annual
Travellers Handbook...
email: cytour@cto.org.cy **www.visitcyprus.com**

get to know the island

THE COUNTRYSIDE

Cyprus has a beautiful and continuously changing panorama which is pure delight for the visitor. Much of the lowland areas of the island are very dry during the summer months but during the spring there is a completely different world to be enjoyed. The island is called *"The Green Jewel of the Mediterranean"*. The countryside is full of green fields with colourful wild flowers and trees laden with blossom. Cyprus is certainly *"The Island of Eternal Beauty"*.

FLORA

Cyprus is extremely interesting and very rich in plants, flowers and shrubs some of which cannot be found anywhere else. This is due to the wide range of climatic conditions. In fact there are more than 1,200 species making this island a botanists paradise. *Some of the most common flowers include:* Anemones - Paparounes (poppies) - Daisies - Tulips - Cyclamen (Kyklamino).

Some of the most common bushes include: Giant Fennel - Oleander (Aphrodaphne) - Myrtle (Myrtia) - Prickly Pear (Papoutsosikia of Francosika)

FAUNA

In pre historic and ancient times the island had a number of wild and rare animals including boars, wild pigs, even leopards, pygmy elephants, genets etc. But Cyprus is most famous for its unique species of wild sheep called Agrinon (Mouflon). It lives in the Paphos mountains around the forest station of Stavros tis Psokas. It is a very shy and swift moving animal, difficult to approach. *Some of the most common inhabitants include:* Goats - Sheep - Donkey -Snakes (black one is harmless, vipers and others are poisonous) - Chameleons and Lizards.

BIRDS OF THE WILD

Cyprus lies in the migration path of many birds which travel from South Africa to the North of Europe and Asia and back including swallows and flamingos. The island is an important place for bird watchers and Khrysochou Bay in Paphos is the most important observatory. There are about 357 species some of which are rare and some only passing through! The Cyprus Ornithological Society, (4, Kanaris Street, Strovolos, Nicosia) keeps records and gives advice and information. (For further reading we highly recommend our fully illustrated, specialist book - **"The Floral Charm of Cyprus"** by Valerie Sinclair. She is an expert on the flora and fauna of the island. It can be found in most book shops.)

NATURE TRAILS
This is the best way to get close to Cyprus' enchanting countryside. The Cyprus Tourism Organisation has organised more than 70 such Trails in rural Cyprus..
Ask for the Special Booklet

Above Left: Spring fields around an ancient monument; Above Right: Village scene in the mountains – The contrasts in the Cyprus countryside are everywhere to be admired.

Above: Berdiga (Chukar)- a colourful bird; Below: The glorious Cyprus Mouflon

Above: Blue Anemone; Below: Cyclamen in the fields, a painting by Renos Lavithis

PLANTS & VEGETABLES

Cyprus has a priceless variety of vegetation. **Vegetables** grow where the land is fertile and there is plenty of water. *They Include:* Tomatoes; Melons; Water Melons; Cucumber; Marrows; Artichokes; Asparagus; Strawberries and many others that can be bought fresh when in season. On the lower slopes of the southern range of Troodos, in the districts of Limassol and Paphos, there are many **vineyards** which produce the famous Cyprus wines.

Fruit. In the lowlands and the hills are to be found the most important and productive **trees** - Almond - Olive and Carob trees. The latter was once called 'the black gold of Cyprus.' All have one characteristic in common - they do not require much care or water. **Citrus.** In good fertile land are: Oranges; Lemons; Grapefruits; Mandarins. Also Figs; Pomegranites.

MAGICAL FOREST

In ancient times the forest was famous and covered vast areas. Over the centuries the wood was used for building the fleets of many major mediterranean countries then forest fires, neglect and the long Turkish occupation (1571-1878) destroyed most of the remaining trees. One of the first things the British administration did after 1878 was to re-establish part of the forest and a programme was started which has continued ever since. In 1974, when Turkey invaded northern Cyprus, their airforce bombed and burned some 15% of the forest but since then the areas destroyed have been replanted. Around 18% of the total area of the island is covered with a variety of trees such as Pine; Cedar; Cypress; Oak; Beech; Eucalyptus etc.

COAST AND THE SEA

Cyprus has an exciting coastline and like the inland landscape it changes from place to place. There are capes, bays, secluded coves, sandy beaches, shingle beaches, exotic rock formations etc. Apart from the popular beaches, there are numerous concealed and deserted ones around the coast which are ideal for escapists.

Marine Life provides over 250 different species of fishes. Fishing in the sea is very popular and for specialists, angling in the reservoirs attracts many anglers.

Underwater Exploration and Diving In the main coastal centres, underwater exploration and Sub Aqua has become very popular. The reefs, the submarine hills, cliffs and valleys are breathtaking. Exotic fish can be seen, corals and other marine plants offer beautiful colours. There can even be some surprises - the discovery of an ancient shipwreck or submerged ancient ruins!

Sailing - Cruising There are regular boat trips from the various ports and harbours along the coast. They are all crewed with experienced, licensed skippers. The island is an ideal place to use as a base from which to enjoy a luxury cruise lasting two or more nights to Egypt or other places in the Eastern Mediterranean.

Sea Sports & Swimming •BLUE FLAG •GREEN - Excellent swimming conditions. • YELLOW - Swim with caution. •RED - Very dangerous - DO NOT ATTEMPT to swim when this flag is flying. • Do not go for a swim straight after a meal or drinking. • Do not cross the boundaries marked by red buoys as you enter areas used by speed boats, fishing boats and other dangerous crafts.

182

Top Left: An old Olive Tree; Above: Almond Tree Blossoms;
Below: Magical Troodos Forest scene

Above Left: Coastline at Protaras-Cape Greco area; Above Right: A diver explores the deep

TO SHOP & BUY

Much of the fun of a holiday in Cyprus is shopping for bargains to take home. In the large towns there are modern shops where shopping is similar to home but in the old quarters of the towns and in the larger villages there are colourful family shops where you can get individual attention and friendly service. Supermarkets also exist in all towns for food, drinks and any other purchases.

The following are renowned regional presents: Local Embroidery (Lefkaritika Lace); Woven items; Needlework; Gold and Silverware; Copper and Brass; Leather Goods; Pottery; Basketwork; Clothes and Shoes; Books and Old Prints; Local Food Specialities; Local Wines and Spirits.

Ideal for Cypriot handicrafts is the **Cyprus Handicraft Service** with branches in major towns. Headquarters in Nicosia: Telephone: 22 30 50 24

Shopping hours are as in other European centres. Usually open at 09am and close between 18.00 to 19.00 hours except Saturday closing at 13.30 and Wednesdays at 14.00. During summer months shops close between 13.00 and 16.00 for a siesta. Sunday closed all day. However, you will find that supermarkets and various shops in Tourist areas extend their opening hours to cater for the visitor's needs.

Above Left: Pots at a local pottery; Above Right: The famous Lefkaritica Lace

Above: Basketwork and trays; Right: Local brandies, wines and sweets

eating out and Cypriot specialities

No holiday in Cyprus is complete without venturing to eat some local delicacies. You can find these in your hotel restaurant or in the traditional restaurants and tavernas which are everywhere. You may like to try an individual dish with a salad or the delicious and filling **Meze**. This is a selection of various local specialities brought to your table over the space of the evening. Being a cosmopolitan place, Cyprus also caters for all eating tastes ranging from British Fish and Chips and fast foods to Chinese, Indian, Italian and other International Cuisine

Whilst on a visit to the island you must not fail to sample some of the local dishes., Just look around for the Taverna that caters for you. Here below, we explain some of the dishes that you may come across on a typical menu. *Enjoy....*

Where to Eat

All tourist places provide a variety of eating places and cuisine.
For traditional local food GO where the locals go. Many of the surrounding villages around the resorts offer local tavernas

What to Eat

There is something for every taste and every pocket. First try MEZE and other local dishes. Do not be surprise to find even Fish & Chips. International and most European Cuisine too.

Where to Drink

In all resorts there are a variety of places to relax. There are Cafe-bars; Coffee bars and Cafes. All providing snacks and drinks.
Bars for an evening out also provide snacks.

the Cyprus Coffee

The Cyprus Coffee is the most popular coffee in the island, a few sips and tasty thick. It is easily noticeable as it is served in tiny cups as:
Sketto (no sugar)
Metrio (medium with bit of sugar)
Glyki (sweet with lots of sugar)
Taste, enjoyable, thick - do not drink the extra grains at the bottom of the cup....

Baked Bread

If you pass near a bakery, do not miss out on a freshly baked loaf of bread. Cypriots like their bread and they put a real art when baking.
The textures and flavours are exceptional, especially the sesame seeds covered loaves.
A bit of fresh bread goes beautifully with a bit of Halloumi, the local cheese....

A table for two by the beach ready for a romantic meal.....or for a more active evening, a Meze meal and an active, entertaining evening.

DIPS - **Taramasalata**: Smoke cod's roe puree; **Tahini**: Sesame seeds pureed into a cream; **Houmous**: Chickpea puree

PASTA - **Ravioles**: Made with cheese or minced meat filling
Pastichion (makaroni tou fournou): Baked macaroni with a minced meat filling and bechamel sauce.

PILAFS - Pougouri: Crushed wheat pilaf with spaghetti

MEAT AND OTHER SPECIALITIES -

Souvlakia: Small pieces of meat on skewered Kebabs cooked over charcoal and served with salad in pitta bread or on the plate.

Sheftalia: Marinated minced meat made into a sausage and cooked on the charcoal.

Loukanika: Spicy meat sausages fried or grilled.

Afelia: Small pieces of pork marinated and cooked slowly in a casserole.

Lountza: Smoked pork fillets, thinly sliced, marinated and served grilled.

Kleftiko: Individually sized pieces of lamb baked very slowly in a Clay oven.

Stifadho: Beef casserole with small onions cooked in red wine.

Moussaka: Layers of potatoes, aubergines, and minced meat covered with bechamel cream and baked in the oven.

Yemista: Dolmadhes, egg plants, tomatoes, marrows stuffed with rice, minced meat and herbs.

Koupepia: Vine leaves stuffed with minced meat and tomato puree; (Dolmadhes)

Koupes: Made of crushed wheat rolls filled with minced meat, onion, parsley and cinnamon, then fried.

Keftedhes: Minced lamb meat balls.

FISH MEALS - Kalamaria: Squid cut in rings or small pieces and fried; **Barbounia**: Red mullet - a tasty fish but with many small bones; **Xyphias**: Sword fish which is usually grilled; **Skaros**: Parrot fish; **Marinadhes**: White bait; **Octapodi** (Octopus): or **squid** cooked or steamed with red wine or served pickled with lemon sauce.

CHEESES - Fetta: White cheese with a sharp, salty taste usually mixed in salad; **Halloumi**: White cheese made from goat's milk; **Anari**: Soft white cheese.

GLYKA (SWEETS) - Kataifi; Baklava; Galatopourekko: Very tasty but very sugary sweets topped with syrup.

Lokoumia: a sweet delicacy - the most famous product of Yeroskipos in Paphos. Usually made with nuts and packed in boxes. Ideal for a present.

Wash down the tasty meals with a nice local wine, either a red or a white, even a rose or try the local beer... Finish with a nice liqueur of **Brandy** *or* **Zivania.**

Brandy Sour

The original Cyprus drink, very refreshing and a speciality everywhere. To prepare: Take a tall glass, sprinkle in some angostura bitters and a good measure of brandy. To follow, add an equal measure of lemon juice, then add sugar (more or less depending on how sweet or sharp you like it), ice cubes, and fill up with soda.

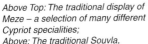

Above Top: The traditional display of Meze – a selection of many different Cypriot specialities;
Above: The traditional Souvla, cooked on charcoal;
Right: Simple fish dishes

THE TASTE OF CYPRUS - A Seasonal Look at Cypriot Cooking...

One of the most popular books on Cyprus Cooking, it will give you a gastro-
nomic experience in preparing and tasting some of the most popular dishes of
the island as prepared by expert cook and writer

GILLI CLIFF

published in full colour and individual recipe illustrations by Topline Publishing

187

index

189

p

r

s

t

v

w

y

explore more about Aphrodite's island through our other publications
www.toplineart.co.uk/publishing
also visit www.renosart.co.uk and www.toplineart.co.uk

Cyprus Main Towns and Villages

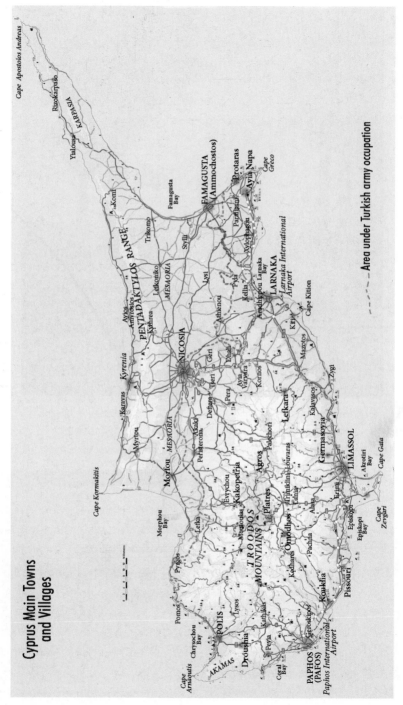

- - - - Area under Turkish army occupation